THE PIF
OF CAYMAN

BY
MARINA CARTER

Pink Pigeon Press

For
Tom Carter
and
Luigi Di Sarno

~

buccaneers in spirit
albeit inhabiting
a less pugnacious era

~

ISBN 0-9539916-2-8

Pink Pigeon Press
92 Greenfield Road
London N15 5ER

Printed and bound in UK

CONTENTS

CARIBBEAN PIRATE HAUNTS

INTRODUCTION

Piracy has been practiced for millennia. The 4,000 year old texts which relate the history of the Sumerian people from the region of modern day Iraq include descriptions of early pirates. Pirates and their captives have for centuries engrossed the popular imagination and are the subject of innumerable books and films. [1]

With the rise in merchant shipping in Europe by 1200, piracy began to take place with official approval, as it came to be recognised that these outlaws of the sea could usefully augment the strength of national fleets. England's first famous pirate was Eustace the Monk, who abandoned the clergy after killing a man in a duel. He raided French ships for England's King John but later changed sides.

The greatest hunting ground in the history of piracy would result from the 1492 discovery of the New World by Christopher Columbus. The Spanish plunder of silver, gold and gems from Mexico and Central and South America produced the largest hoard of treasure ever shipped across the seas up to that time. [2]

The route used by pirates who travelled from Caribbean bases to the Indian Ocean and the Red Sea to plunder shipping, before returning to sell goods to colonists in North America, became known as the **pirate round**, and its heyday was the thirty year period between 1690 and 1720.

An early victim of pirates was **Julius Caesar,** captured in the Aegean around 75 BC. A ransom was demanded for his release.

CORSAIRS, PRIVATEERS, BUCCANEERS AND PIRATES

Individuals and groups who perpetrated attacks on sea-going vessels, with the tacit consent of their governments, or as outcastes and outlaws, have been characterised by a variety of labels. Frenchmen from Normandy and Brittany were among the first of the northern maritime nations to plunder Spanish argosies returning from the New World. They were known as **corsairs**. [3]

Increasingly, such individuals sailed under royal commission and legal protection. They carried 'letters of marque', authorising them to capture vessels belonging to hostile nations and became known as **privateers**. However, the encouragement of privateering at times of war could spell trouble in periods of peace, when men who had become accustomed to the thrills and profits of privateering might be tempted into plunder for its own sake. Thus it was that scores of disaffected soldiers and sailors, or ill-treated indentured servants, became renegades, settling on deserted islands and secluded coasts.

Furthermore, the distinction between the authorised privateers and the outlaws of the sea who were called **pirates**, depended on one's perspective. English privateers, even as distinguished a man as Francis Drake, would have been considered pirates by the Spanish and vice versa. Notorious pirates often started their careers as privateers, and would often attempt to disguise their piracy by claiming only to capture foreign ships. Piracy became a particular problem after 1603, when 50 years of Anglo-Spanish fighting ended, and again after 1713 when the Peace of Utrecht was signed, and 40,000 Royal Navy sailors were discharged.

Buccaneering in the Caribbean is conventionally dated from about 1640, when bands of rovers from the recently settled British and French islands in the outer Antilles established themselves in locations along Spanish trade routes where they could obtain supplies in between hijackings. These renegades initially established themselves along the northern coast of Hispaniola where they formed small hunting communities. The **buccaneers** were so known after their method of smoking or 'boucaner' the hogs and cattle which they sold to passing ships. Around the middle of the 17th century, however, driven off Hispaniola, the buccaneers settled on Tortuga, a nearby island, where they established a republic with a fort and transformed themselves from hunters of cattle into hunters of men. [4]

A FRENCH BUCCANEER
(as depicted in P. Christian, *Histoire des Pirates*, 1850).

THE CARIBBEAN IN THE 17TH AND 18TH CENTURIES

Once Spanish, Portuguese and Italian navigators had charted routes to the New World in the second half of the 15th century, trade in exotic products and slaves became highly profitable. And where treasure ships sailed, pirates and privateers inevitably followed. The Spanish were primarily interested in the precious metals which could be mined in the New World, and over the course of the 16th century, they carried home the equivalent of 3 times the total European stock of gold and silver. [5]

By the 17th century, however, Spanish domination was being challenged by arriving settlers. From the 1620s English settlers moved onto St Christopher (St Kitts), Barbados, Nevis and Antigua. The French and Dutch also established themselves in the Caribbean, with the latter occupying Curacao, Bonair and Aruba. Spanish dominion, confirmed by the Papal Bull of 1493, was under threat, and they regarded the English, French and Dutch in the region as interlopers. Not only could these nations launch raids from their settlements against the rich towns of the Spanish Main, they spawned buccaneers – men who had escaped from persecution at home, and from forced labour on ships and farms overseas - to become the feared **flibustiers** or freebooters of the West Indies. With men of these northern nations established on islands in the Antilles, the Spanish became ever more vulnerable as their heavily laden homeward bound fleets traversed the Caribbean Sea. In 1655 the English established an even more threatening presence in the Caribbean, capturing Jamaica from the Spanish. Buccaneers, driven from their habitual haunts by the Spanish, could now take refuge in Jamaica, swelling the ranks of discharged and mutinous soldiers and sailors who were willing recruits for privateers and for pirate cruises.

The Spanish treasure route was vulnerable to attack at several points. Precious metals mined by the Spanish in Mexico and Peru were generally transported, at this time, by mule trains and coastal vessels

PRIVATEERS ATTACKING PORTOBELLO
(Exquemelin, A.O. Boucaniers of America, 1684)

to ports such as Veracruz, Cartagena, and Portobello. Drake targeted mule trains transporting bullion across the isthmus of Panama while Morgan and other privateers launched daring raids on key towns of the Spanish Main such as Portobello, and Maracaibo.

The attitude of local governors in the Caribbean settlements to the presence and activities of privateers was ambivalent. The colonies were ooorly defended in these early years, and privateers could provide a welcome source of defence to counteract the raids and threats of hostile nations. At the same time, its encouragement merely served to escalate the attacks and counter-attacks which troubled sea-borne trade in the region, while raising an army of plunderers could prove doubly counter-productive when some of them turned to piracy, and began to attack their own side.

Thus when Thomas Modyford was appointed Governor of Jamaica in 1664, despite having instructions to warn privateers against attacking Spanish ships, he feared that they would go over to the French, and decided to lend tacit support to their raids against Campeche in Mexico, Isla de Providencia off Nicaragua, and Puerto Principe in Cuba. Henry Morgan's attacks on Portobello (Panama) and Maracaibo (Venezuela) in 1668-9 were ostensibly provoked by rumours that the Spanish intended to attack Jamaica.

The ambivalence of administrators can be seen from their characterisation of privateers as 'dangerous rogues' whilst avowedly hoping by 'gentleness' to limit their raids to authorised targets. In 1666, deliberating on the question of privateering, the Council of Jamaica acknowledged that granting letters of marque to privateers to attack the Spanish was both economically and politically desirable: it would furnish the island with necessary goods, stimulate trade, check Spanish designs on English territory and above all was seen to be *the only means to keep the buccaneers on Hispaniola, Tortuga, and the South and North Quays of Cuba from being their enemies and infesting their seaside plantations*. [6]

In 1671, however, the new Governor of Jamaica, Sir Thomas Lynch, voiced his very real concerns about the privateers:

> *Privateering encourages all manner of disorder and dissoluteness, and if it succeeded does but enrich the worst sort of people, and provoke and alarm the Spaniards, constraining them to arm and fortify.*

By the following year, he reported that he had drastically reduced their number.

If Jamaica and other Caribbean islands succeeded in reducing the numbers of privateers operating from their ports, other havens soon opened up to them, however. In 1684, Lynch decried the retreats offered to privateers in Carolina, and New England, whose colonists, he reported, "are now full of pirates' money". [7]

In practice, successful privateers could always aspire to become respected planters once their roving days were over, while Caribbean administrators vacillated between reeling in pirates with pardons or pursuing them relentlessly.

In 1713, with the ending of the war of Spanish Succession, England, at peace with both Spain and France, could no longer indulge in legitimate privateering. Numbers of men, accustomed to the lifestyle of plunder, now ostensibly without employment, turned to piracy. Thus began what was to become the most notorious few years in Caribbean history, when pirates like Blackbeard roamed the seas. During these years the sight of the severed heads of such outlaws hanging from the bowsprit of naval vessels or dangling on the gallows at Negrils Point on Jamaica became all too familiar. Most of these notorious men had been rounded up and executed within a couple of decades, but as late as 1795 Jamaica was still complaining about the activities of privateers. [8]

PIRATE HAUNTS IN THE CARIBBEAN

The numerous isles and islets of the Caribbean provided refuges, hide-aways and safe havens for the flotsam and jetsam of humanity – runaway sailors and apprentices, adventurers and exiles – who washed up on its shores. Small uninhabited islands with secluded coves made ideal hide-outs for pirates who would lie in wait for passing merchant ships and stop to refit, careen their ships and take on water between voyages of plunder. Pirate safe havens also developed where the facilities of a sheltered natural harbour, well fortified with cannon, were joined with warehouses and taverns. Here booty could be traded and loot spent, carpenters were on hand to repair ships, and medical help available to casualties of boarding parties and pitched battles on the high seas. [9]

Hispaniola and its islets

The northern coast of Hispaniola was occupied by buccaneers from the early 17th century. Considered an irritant by the Spanish, they were driven off the mainland to the neighbouring island of **Tortuga** where they set up an outlaw outpost. Controlled and fortified by a French Huguenot, Levasseur, in the 1640s, the buccaneers suffered a series of raids, but maintained a foothold on Tortuga until driven away by the Spanish in 1653. The islet continued to serve as a rendezvous for privateers seeking commissions from whoever would entertain them, and to be disputed by the English and the French, but following the take-over of Jamaica by the English, many buccaneers were encouraged to bring their prizes to Port Royal, on the latter island, which was developing into the Caribbean's premier safe haven for freebooters. **Petit Goave** and **Isle a Vaches**, off Hispaniola, also served as refuges for privateers and buccaneers. [10]

Port Royal

Jamaica's southern coast became the new resort of freebooters who had formerly made Hispaniola and Tortuga their headquarters. The rump of Cromwell's troops swelled the numbers of privateers operating from Port Royal, launching attacks on Spanish ships, and returning with booty to Jamaica. The heyday of privateering in Port Royal was between 1657 and 1671 when huge profits were made in attacks on Spanish territory and ships, and the men involved in them played a crucial role in the power struggle with Spain. It was from here in 1664, that the raids against Campeche, Isla de Providencia, and Puerto Principe were launched. Henry Morgan also organised his notorious privateering expeditions to Panama and Venezuela from Port Royal in 1668 and 1669.

Between 1671 and 1680, privateering took on a surreptitious character, as it was officially discouraged but privately supported. After 1680, the freebooters and adventurers who had played an important role in securing Port Royal against Spanish attack, were no longer in favour, and piracy was increasingly seen as a scourge to be rooted out.[11]

Port Royal's nemesis came on 7 June 1692 when part of the city collapsed into the sea as the result of a massive earthquake. It has been estimated that around 2,000 of the inhabitants were killed by the quake and accompanying tidal wave. Befitting its status as a haunt of outlaws, the city and its floating corpses were looted by the surviving pirates. The event was viewed by many as God's vengeance against the debauchery of what had been the most notorious pirate hangout in the Americas. In the early 18th century, Port Royal purged its pirate legacy with the public execution of some of the most vilified outlaws of the day, at Gallows Point, a low promontory, east of the city. [12]

New Providence

The island of Providence in the Bahamas (modern day Nassau) achieved notoriety in the early 18th century when it was used as a base by pirates such as Calico Jack Rackham who briefly terrorised the Caribbean before being rounded up and executed. The century started inauspiciously on Providence, when the eruption of the Spanish War of Succession led to renewed hostilities in the Caribbean, with French flibustiers now reluctant allies of the Spanish against the English. In 1703 Providence was razed to the ground by French and Spanish marauders, and the inhabitants "all put to the sword or carried off". [13] By the time peace was declared in 1713, a new generation of privateers had emerged, and once again, significant numbers refused to renounce a life of plunder. They sought refuge in the Bahamas, temporarily uninhabited after repeated attacks, and strategically located. The port of New Providence was found to be *"especially well suited to their purposes: its harbour was too shallow and tricky for heavy men-of-war to enter easily, while the surrounding hills afforded excellent vantage points for espying passing ships"*. [14] With abundant game, fish, fruit and fresh water, several hundred buccaneers found the archipelago an attractive centre of operations. By 1716, New Providence was being described as "a nest of pirates", as notorious pirate commanders like Charles Vane and Benjamin Hornigold harassed merchant ships travelling to and from the Caribbean. [15]

Royal Navy cruisers found it difficult to flush out the pirates from their New Providence lair, and accordingly it was left to a consortium of London merchants to take the Bahamas in hand. Leasing the islands from the crown, they sent out an experienced sea captain, and former privateer, Woodes Rogers, to take charge of the island, and declare war on the pirates. Meanwhile, the British government was also waving a flag of truce at the pirates by offering them royal pardons. In December 1717 a sloop had been sent by Governor Bennett of Bermuda to inform the several hundred pirates based on New Providence of this opportunity to surrender. Several took up the offer but by March 1718 Bennett was gloomily reporting that the pirates *"declare they will never surrender without the assurance of enjoying what they have gotten, for otherwise say we have ventured our necks for nothing"* .By May, the situation had deteriorated,

WOODES ROGERS, 1729

and the Governor noted that the safety of his own territory had been threatened, the pirates having sent him word that *"when the men of war cruses upon them amongst the Bahama Islands, they will joyn all the forces they can and come and take this country"*. [16]

Woodes Rogers was sailing into an explosive situation, and when his flagship, accompanied by frigates and sloops arrived off New Providence, the pirates were ready. Charles Vane set light to a recently captured French ship, and allowed it to drift towards the frigates as they approached the harbour. At dawn Vane fluttered his black pirate flag at the waiting fleet and steered out to open sea, dodging his naval pursuers. However, this impressive act of defiance was not equalled ashore. When Woodes Rogers finally made land on 27 July, the remaining pirates welcomed him and more than 600 accepted the royal pardons offered. The 'nest of pirates' had been stamped upon, but the Caribbean was not purged of this scourge for several more years, as the more notorious of Providence's outlaws – including the infamous Blackbeard – had already left to continue their depredations elsewhere.

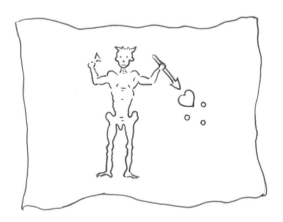

BLACKBEARD'S PIRATE FLAG

THE PLACE OF THE CAYMAN ISLANDS
IN PIRATE HISTORY

Not discovered until the early 16th century when Colmbus, on his
fourth voyage of exploration, sighted the smaller islands, Cayman
remained for many years only sporadically inhabited. This, of course,
made the region an ideal pirate haunt.

The most prolonged and dangerous of Columbus' epic journeys, the
fourth voyage included an exploration of the Western Caribbean.
The fleet set sail from Cadiz on 9 May 1502. By 15 June they were
at Martinique, but steering a course through the Caribbean, they were
caught in a hurricane. The fleet sheltered in a small harbour and then
made for Puerto Escondido on the south side of Hispaniola.

After visiting and describing various points of Central America and
its 'Indian' inhabitants, and suffering an attack which killed several,
Columbus had set out to return to Hispaniola when he unwittingly
came in sight of the Lesser Caymans. His son, Ferdinand described the
incident in his journal: "*on Wednesday 10 May we were in sight of two
very small and low islands, full of turtles; all the sea about there was
so full of them that they looked like little rocks, and for this
reason those islands were called Las Tortugas*". [17]

Despite Columbus' discovery, the Spanish showed no inclination to
settle on Cayman. Spanish Captain Don Juan Tirri later explained this
as due to Grand Cayman's "diminutive size" which, "*in comparison
with the vast territories which ever since the age of discoveries have
claimed the attention of our Government, doubtless explains why it
has been entirely neglected*". Nonetheless, the Cayman Islands served
as important landmarks for the Spanish convoys bound for Mexico.
Entering the Caribbean Sea at the Lesser Antilles, they used Cayman
to guide them away from the treacherous coasts of southern Cuba. The
treasure convoys which sailed north from Cartagena to Havana also
headed towards the Cayman Islands. [18]

**A YOUTHFUL
COLUMBUS
ON HIS FIRST
VOYAGE**

**COLUMBUS'
FLEET**

J. Abbot, *Life and Achievements of Christopher Columbus*, 1879.

Over succeeding years, however, the Cayman Islands slowly gained recognition for more than their strategic location. By the mid 1600s the Dutch and French were familiar with the timing of annual turtle migrations, and regularly anchored off the shores of Grand and Little Cayman to provision their ships. The French, by the mid 17th century, had even established a seasonal settlement on Cayman, spending a month or two each year slaughtering and salting the turtles that came ashore to lay their eggs. [19]

Almost as soon as the English had established a foothold in the Caribbean, they were relying on the Cayman Islands as a source of food, and by the 1660s, it was becoming evident that the islands needed to be defended as an integral part of British interests in the region. [20] At the same time, Cayman was itself attracting a class of sojourner not entirely to the liking of the British authorities. In August 1671, a proclamation called upon the *"soldiers, planters, privateers, and other late inhabitants of this island now at Caimanos, Musphitos, Keys and other remote places"* to return to Jamaica. [21] This constitutes the first official recognition that privateers and others were making use of the Cayman Islands, but it is clear that they had been of interest to outlaws, runaways and renegades for some time.

As succeeding sections of this book will show, Cayman was visited by numerous privateers en route to and returning from their voyages of plunder. Drake, Dampier, Morgan and many other famous names stopped to provision, rest or hide out on these islands. Dutch, French and Spanish privateers and corsairs were all familiar with Cayman. It was in 1669 that the corsair Rivero Pardal had launched his notorious attack on Cayman settlers, while in 1677, it was reported that Dutch privateers, who had burnt French ships off Hispaniola and taken Curacao, had gone to the Cayman islands with booty which included 500 negroes and 28lbs of gold.[22]

Cayman was attractive to privateers and pirates for a number of reasons. First and foremost were the supplies of turtle which could be found on Cayman for a limited season each year, starting around May, when females would come on shore to lay their eggs. They would be stalked by night, and by the simple expedient of turning them on their backs, sailors could leave them helpless till the following day, when they would return to slaughter and pack the valuable meat. Sir Hans Sloane, a noted medical man and naturalist, who visited Cayman Brac in March 1677, reported seeing there "some huts for the turtlers, or those who catch the turtle or tortoises", and stated of the Cayman Islands in general that they and their produce were believed to have restorative qualities: *"These low Islands are very much frequented by Turtlers from Jamaica, who go thither to catch the Tortoises, that come to lay their Eggs in the Sand, and are taken by those who make it their Trade. 'Tis commonly thought that a Voyage and staying on these Islands for some time, feeding only upon Turtle, cures the Pox".*[23] After British troops had taken Jamaica from the Spanish, the soldiers depended heavily on supplies of turtle brought from Cayman, and traders continued to leave Port Royal each season to pick up this meat which played a large part in Jamaican cooking for many years. [24]

Alongside the sought-after turtle meat, the Cayman Islands, with their reefs and secluded harbours, provided a protective haven, a place to water, careen their ships, and rest, for outlaws of every description. Furthermore, strategically located, as the islands were, on the trade routes, they were an ideal location in which to lay in wait for passing merchantmen. The low lying islands were difficult to spot at night, and depth soundings were complicated by a sudden rise in the seafloor. [25] Outlaws, frequenting the region, could take advantage of ships which came to grief on the treacherous reefs, to strip the helpless vessels of their cargoes. Privateers also used Cayman as a rendezvous point, or to stop off and distribute their booty after successful expeditions. [26]

REFERENCES

1. S. Johnson, *Sunken Ships and Treasures*, p. 365.
2. ibid., p. 366-7.
3. C. Haring, *The Buccaneers in the West Indies in the XVII Century*, p. 13.
4. R.S. Smith, *The Maritime Heritage of the Cayman Islands*, p. 89 and see J. S. Bromley, *Corsairs and Navies, 1660-1760*.
5. J. Ure, *The Quest for Captain Morgan*, p 24 –6.
6. Calendar of State Papers, America and West Indies, [CSP] 1661-68 no 767, 30 June 1664.
7. CSP no 934 12 Feb 1665; no 942 20 Feb 1665, no 1138 22 Feb 1666, and CSP1669-1674 no 697 17 Dec 1671.
8. PRO CO 137/95 Robert Sewell, Agent for Jamaica to Duke of Portland, 1 June 1795.
9. M. Oliver, *Blackbeard and his murderous mateys*, p. 72-3.
10. C. Haring, op.cit., p. 80-83
11. M. Pawson, & D. Buisseret, D. *Port Royal, Jamaica*, p. 36. See also Smith, op. cit., p 82-3.
12. S. Johnson, op. cit., p. 369.
13. PRO CO 5/3 Weymouth to the Earl of Nottingham, 11 Dec 1703.
14. D. Marley, *Pirates. Adventurers of the High Seas*, p. 130-1.
15. CSP 1716 Spottswood to Council of Trade and Plantations, July 1716.
16. CSP 1717- 1718 Nos 345, 384, 471, 474 and 551. Lt Governor Bennett, Feb to May 1718.
17. Morison, S.E. *Journals and Other Documents on the Life and Voyages of Christopher Columbus*, p. 307, 353.
18. Smith, op. cit., p. 57, 148.
19. Laet, J. *History of the West Indies*, vol 1, p 42; Smith, op. cit., p. 60-61.
20. CSP 1661-68 no 164 27 Aug 1661; and see Hirst, *Notes on the History of the Cayman Islands*, p. 17 and Smith,op. cit., p. 63-4.
21. CSP 1669-1674 no 552 Minutes of the Council of Jamaica, 12 Aug 1671.
22. CSP 1677-1680 no 313 26 June 1677 Vaughan to Coventry.
23. Sloane, H. *A Voyage to the Islands ...,* vol 1.
24. Pawson, M. & Buisseret, D., op. cit., p. 67.
25. Smith, R.S., op. cit., p. 148-9.
26. See for example, CSP 1681-1685 no 1163 Sir Thomas Lynch to Secretary Sir Leoline Jenkins, 26 July 1683.

CHAPTER ONE
THE PIRATE LIFESTYLE

Our impression of pirates has been fed by glamorised films and literary depictions. We visualise swashbuckling, moustachioed gallants, in brightly coloured costumes. Among them will be, invariably, an old seafarer with gnarled features and a wooden leg, a beloved parrot perched on his shoulder. Pirates of the popular kind have catch-phrases: 'Ahoy me hearties!', and customs – walking the plank – which are legendary. But are they accurate? What kind of men turned to piracy? Who were the buccaneers who reputedly settled in and around Cayman? And why were some of the men who looted and plundered subsequently feted as national heroes, honoured and enriched, while others, reviled, were summarily executed or festered in dark dungeons?

PIRATE RECRUITS - THE REALITY

The typical pirate was an experienced mariner who had been discharged or had deserted from merchant or naval service. Men press-ganged into taking naval service, or who had been embittered by the harsh discipline of ship-board life, might consider escape to the relative egalitarianism of a pirate vessel a preferable option. They might also subsequently enact revenge on fellow mariners or officers who had ill-treated them. For example, when Alexander Gilmore, a mariner from the HMS Phoenix, and who was on board the 'John and Elizabeth' when it was taken by 2 pirate sloops, was spotted by one of their number, Robert Hudson, a deserter from the Phoenix, he turned on Gilmore, cocking his pistol at him and saying *"Damn your Blood, I'll kill you, for sending me on the Main Yard in the Storm"*. Gilmore was only saved due to the intervention of the pirate commander.

THE PIRATE
IN POPULAR LITERATURE

I wish I was a pirate
With a long beard hanging down,
A cutlass dangling from my belt
My teeth all black and brown.

'I wish I was a pirate'
by Tony Bradman in
Pirate Poems ed J. Foster, OUP, 1991

PIRATE DRESS

Pirates probably wore the dress of sailors of their time - short blue jackets over a check shirt, and long canvas trousers or baggy breeches.

They are often depicted wearing weapons, particularly with a brace or more of pistols and brandishing a cutlass.

The log of HMS Adventure, which was cruising in Caribbean waters in 1767-1769, details incidents illustrative of navy life and which reveal routine punishments meted out to misbehaving mariners. Even on the last day of the voyage, as the ship returned to Port Royal in Jamaica, on 31 August 1769, that day's entry was full of brutality: *"punished Valentine Powell marine for getting drunk and quarrelling when on his post, William Johnson marine for insolence to the Captain with a dozen lashes each, Mathew Williams seaman ran the gauntlet for theft"*. Running the gauntlet was a particularly nasty punishment devised for those in naval service. If a man committed a petty larceny or some such offence against his fellow sailors he could be punished by having to 'run the gauntlet' of the entire assembled crew, who would strike him in turn. [1]

Recruits were also gleaned from the less fortunate members of
colonial society – indentured servants who were condemned to work
for low wages in return for their passage out, petty criminals and the
flotsam and jetsam of adventurers who found their way to the
embryonic Caribbean 17th century settlements. One of the most
famous of buccaneers, and a chronicler of their exploits against the
Spanish, Alexander Olivier Exquemelin, had himself arrived in
Tortuga in 1666 as an 'engage' of the French West India Company.
Possibly of Flemish or Dutch origin, and born around 1654, he was
one of many young men of poor family who chanced their lot in
colonial service and lived to regret it. After serving several years with
a cruel master, he ran away to become a buccaneer. His narrative,
published in the 17th century, records

> *We set sail from France in a ship called the St John on the second
> day of May, 1666. The ship carried 28 guns and 20 seamen, as well
> as 220 passengers, including indentured servants and free persons
> with their servants … We reached Tortuga on the 7th day of July
> 1666 … The pirates, hunters and planters of Tortuga promised to buy
> their necessities from the Company, and were given them on credit.
> The Company soon found that they could not get either payment, or
> the return of their goods from those people, not even by bringing in
> armed men. So the Company told their factors to sell up everything
> that the Company owned, even the servants belonging to the
> Company and all other goods. I was also sold, as a servant of the
> said Company, in whose service I came out of France. I was unlucky.
> I fell into the hands of a cruel tyrant, the Lieutenant General of the
> island. This man treated me cruelly; I thought I would die of hunger.
> … At last I grew very sick, and my master feared I would die. Fearing
> that this would mean that he had no profit from the money he had
> given for me, he sold me to a surgeon for 70 pieces of eight. With him
> I began to recover my health, as he was kind to me. He gave me
> clothes and very good food, and after I had served him for just a year
> he gave me my freedom, on a promise that I would pay him 100
> pieces of eight as soon as I was able. I was now free, but had nothing,
> and did not know how to make my living, so I decided to join the
> wicked order of pirates or robbers at sea. I was accepted into this
> society and stayed with them until 1672.* [2]

In 1684 the Governor of Jamaica confirmed that men under indenture
were tempted into joining privateering ventures:

> *All servants that can, run away and turn pirates encouraged by the*
> *late successes ... The captains of the men-of-war formerly had orders*
> *to take the King's subjects out of foreign and wrecked vessels, but now*
> *the Admiralty orders none such to be victualled, so it is not to be done.*
> *I am sorry that the King's necessities should require this order, for it*
> *will lose him many subjects.* [3]

His comments demonstrate that victims of shipwreck or capture by
hostile nations might themselves also be a prey to be recruited onto
privateer or pirate vessels, through sheer necessity.

Unwilling recruits into piracy, who had themselves been captured,
or pressed into serving, were particularly likely to have skills prized
by the outlaws. Thus, a ship's carpenter or cooper who was unlucky
enough to be stopped by pirates might find himself under considerable
pressure to sign the pirate 'articles' and come away with them.
Joan Boys was forced to work for Spanish privateers after they
discovered that he was an experienced pilot around the South Cays. [4]
Such professional seafarers possessed the skills to outwit pursuers and
a knowledge of reefs, cays and far flung ports. A successful pirate
cruise depended on the ability to attack, escape, survive in hiding,
and emerge to strike again.

LIFE ABOARD A PIRATE SHIP

Once the pirate crew had been assembled (whether voluntarily or not)
individuals would be required to embark any goods required for the
voyage, particularly gunpowder and shot. Generally pork and turtle
meat was acquired and salted. Sometimes food was obtained by
robbery. A meeting would then be held to decide where to go.

Despite the roguish character of piratical activities, their lives were
governed by specific regulations. Pirate crews generally drew up a list
of rules known as **Articles**. These usually detailed how any booty
would be divided, established a code of conduct for crews, and

penalties for infringement. In 1720 Gorge Lowther's crew apportioned their loot, according to agreement, with a double share going to the captain, a 1.5 share to the ship's master, and a 1.25 share going to the doctor, mate and gunner respectively.

The Articles might even offer some form of insurance for the pirates, providing details of compensation in the event of injuries sustained in the battles which would inevitably ensue with the objects of their depredations. Exquemelin reported that the recompense offered to his crew in the event of being wounded was as follows:

> For the loss of a right arm, 600 pieces of eight or six slaves; for the loss of a left arm, 500 pieces of eight or five slaves; for a right leg, 500 pieces of eight or five slaves; for the left leg, 400 pieces of eight or four slaves; for an eye, 100 pieces of eight or one slave; for a finger the same as for an eye. All is paid from the common stock.

He also asserted that the pirates behaved generously towards each other and even to their prisoners – putting them ashore as soon as possible, and only keeping them "*if they need servants, who they will release after two or three years*". [5]

There was also a form of hierarchy on board the pirate ship. The most famous of the pirates, like Blackbeard and Calico Jack Rackham, were usually also the commanders or captains of the ships which they brought into this notorious service. They would be assisted by a 'quartermaster', just as on a naval vessel. This officer would be responsible for disciplining the crew, could order floggings and other punishments and, where necessary, might even turn a turbulent sailor off the vessel to languish on some lonely shore. [6]

In many respects, shipboard life for a pirate resembled that of an ordinary seaman. There were the usual tasks of maintaining and operating the vessel, repairs to be carried out, decks to be cleaned, sails to be rigged and so on. However, the pirate deckhand would also be expected to combine the ability to caulk the boat and repair sails with good fighting skills. The job of the look-out might be enlivened on board a pirate ship by the promise that the first to spot a potential victim's sail from the rigging or crow's nest would receive the best pistol found on board the prize. The ship's carpenter could find that he was expected to double up as the surgeon, using his saw not only on planks but to amputate the limbs of his wounded ship-mates. 7

The quartermaster had no easy job. Men who had risked their all to join a pirate ship, and knowing that capture was as good as a death their dangerous choice worthwhile. If a pirate captain showed reluctance to go after a well-armed merchantman, a crew might well rise up in mutiny and vote to overthrow him, appointing a more daring leader in his place. This is, in fact, how Jack Rackham came to prominence.

PIRATE ATTACKS

With the crew on board and provisions assembled the search could begin for prizes. In general, pirates and privateers looked for fast and easily manoeuvrable craft. Privateers like Francis Drake favoured caravels, while pirates often converted small sloops and schooners which they had themselves captured and subsequently armed. 8 Occasionally, pirates captured a larger man-of-war and joined forces to create a fleet of formidable proportions and power. But more usually, commanding smaller vessels, and often acting alone or in twos and threes, they relied on surprise, speed and cunning to pounce on their victims.

It was not unheard of for pirates to trick ships into approaching them. Pirate vessels always carried a disproportionately high number of men (so as to overwhelm opposing crews) and might conceal some of their number below decks while disguising others as women, in order to convince passing ships of their inoffensive character.

Swooping in on relatively poorly armed merchantmen, or even defenceless fishing sloops, pirates used the minimum fire power necessary while employing to maximum effect the elements of fear

A WEST INDIAN BRIGANTINE
(Labat, *Nouveau Voyage aux Iles,* 1727)

A TYPICAL SAILING CRAFT WHICH
WOULD HAVE BEEN USED BY A PIRATE

JACK RACKHAM'S
PIRATE FLAG

Pirate vessels carried a range of flags to deceive their victims into thinking they represented friendly nations. Once the prizes had been lured to close range, the pirates would unfurl their skull and crossbones, unleash their guns or brandish their weapons as they homed in on their prey.

and shock which their sudden and awesome appearance could provoke. They used all the means at their disposal to terrify opponents: from fearsome flags, to blood-curdling screams. Their countenances and dress were altered to heighten the effect:

Blackbeard was reputed to place smoking matches beneath his unruly hair and beard to give him an even more frightening appearance.

BLACKBEARD
(Johnson, *A History of the Pyrates*, 1724)

It was the level of violence used by pirate crews which determined their notoriety. Whilst some pirates treated their victims with relative courtesy, simply holding them until the ship had been looted and then allowing them to depart with their vessel, others subjected their unfortunate captives to all manner of indignities, humiliations and occasionally torture.

Harrowing depositions of sailors and traders reveal bloody scenes in which hapless captains were mutilated and killed as pirates attempted to ascertain the whereabouts on board of suspected caches of money and valuables. Pirates who had been in naval service might likewise exact revenge on their former superiors or officers known for their sadistic disciplining of sailors by subjecting them to unspeakable tortures and miserable deaths. Edward North, a sailor intercepted by the pirate Charles Vane reported that the latter had

> *barbarously treated the deponent with all his company by beating them and using other cruelties, particularly to one, who they bound hands and feet and ty'd (upon his back) down to the bowsprit with Matches to his eyes burning and a pistol loaded with the muzzle into his mouth, thereby to oblige him to confess what money was on board.*

INTERROGATING A CAPTIVE
(R. de La Croix, *Histoire de la Piraterie*)

EXQUEMELIN ON PIRATE TORTURE :

The pirates would torture people to make them say where other people were hiding, or where their goods were hidden. They put them to the rack and beat them with sticks. Others had burning matches placed between their fingers, while others had cords twisted about their heads until their eyes stood out of their heads. Even if they had nothing to confess they died of these inhuman tortures ... Some were crucified. Others had their feet stuck in a fire, and were burned alive. They would do this to white men and their Negro slaves, with equal cruelty. [9]

John Shattock had good cause to regret that on 3 Oct 1718, having sailed from Jamaica bound for Salem, he met a pirate brigantine of 12 guns commanded by Charles Vane who hoisted a black flag and fired a shot at him

> *on board he was much beat and abused by Charles Vane to force him to discover if he had any money on board his vessel, on complaining to Deal of his hard usage, Deal replied 'Damn you, you old Dog, then tell where your Money is; ... if we find you in one Lye, we'll Damn you and your Vessel also', later that day, the pirates let him depart.* [10]

PIRATE BOOTY

In practice, it was not only the treasure ships of the Spanish fleet or the silks and spices carried by wealthy Indiamen which attracted pirates. The buccaneers made their living from the cattle they rounded up on inland raids, selling the meat and hides to passing ships. Pirates were likewise interested in looting the stores carried by ships.

Almost anything found on board a captured vessel could be considered as booty: slaves would be rounded up and either recruited into the pirate crew if hands were needed or traded at a nearby port, wealthy or notable passengers could be held, to be ransomed.

EXAMINING NEWLY
ACQUIRED LOOT

Ships carrying cargoes of sugar, tobacco and even coal were also seen as useful targets - the goods could be traded, with a portion set aside for the pirates' own use. Even the ropes, sails and charts of the ships would be looted, as these were always handy. Medical supplies might be particularly valued by pirates, whose fearsome profession brought a high casualty rate. Blackbeard once blockaded Charleston harbour, causing massive disruption to trade, for no better reason than that he was urgently in need of medicines for his crew. [11]

Pirates' bravado in pursuing a ship and in boarding it once within close range was often fuelled by alcohol. And, if the raid was a success, the rum and wine found on board a prize was commonly among the first items to be liberally indulged in by the pirates. Their carousing was legendary, and if the spoils were great, vast sums of money obtained from goods sold as booty were likely to be expended in the taverns and brothels of pirate haunts such as Port Royal on Jamaica. Fortunes so easily acquired, could as easily be squandered, and within a few weeks, the crews, their money exhausted, would be clamouring to set sail in search of more treasure.

A FINE DIVIDING LINE: NOTORIOUS PIRATES AND ILLUSTRIOUS PRIVATEERS

Not all of those men who commanded ships which plundered on the high seas have been represented to history in the same light as the brutal desperados who met their end, like Captain Kidd, swinging from a gibbet overlooking the Thames. Pirates who might be seen as the public enemy number one by some nations, could be feted by others. Thus while British history books taught schoolchildren for generations that Francis Drake was a hero, richly rewarded and idolised, for the Spanish he was an archetypal villain: just 'El Draque', the notorious pirate.

Privateers were commissioned to attack the ships and bases of hostile nations, and, whilst effectively, in many cases, enriching themselves, were in principle supposed to hand over their plunder to the benefit of their nation and sovereign. Elizabeth I of England thus gained handsomely by Drake's efforts, while Henry Morgan's daring assaults on the Spanish Main, despite provoking some disquiet over the extent of pillage and murder committed, were ultimately viewed as a great achievement and duly recognised in his nomination to the Deputy Governorship of Jamaica.

The fine line between privateering and piracy, when viewed from the point of view of opposing nations, could be overstepped by men unable to resist the temptation of plundering ships and ports for which they had no commission, and even those of their own compatriots. It was not uncommon for the Governors of Caribbean islands to find themselves forced to hunt down privateers sent out on commissions, who had subsequently turned pirate and become a threat to their own side. In 1664, for example, the Governor of Jamaica reported that he had dispatched a ketch to Hispaniola to apprehend John Moro, a Frenchman and captain of the 'St Louis' frigate whose commission from Lord Windsor against the Spanish having expired, "*turned pirate and tooke an Hampton man bound hither whose men came down in a sloope complayning much of their hard fortune*". Captain Ensom was sent after the privateers with 60 men in the 'Swallow'. Finding Moro's ship at anchor, Ensom engaged him in a battle, during which Moro, another pirate named Grand Luis, and a number of the crew were killed. The rest were taken prisoner and brought back to Jamaica. Subsequently, 14 of the pirates were captured, found guilty and sentenced to death. They were hanged at Port Royal and St Jago, on Jamaica. [12]

PIRATE HUNTERS

Captain Ensom, and the innumerable naval officers sent in pursuit of pirates, are the real heroes of this dramatic era. yet all too often the glory and the notoriety is given to the villains rather than the men of service who courageously hunted them down. Cruising the dangerous waters of the Caribbean, naval commanders could be summarily ordered by the administrators of the troubled colonies to set off in pursuit of barbaric pirates or their own unruly privateers. The instructions given to Captain Mitchell, a Royal Navy officer aboard HMS Ruby, by Colonel Hender Molesworth on 23 November 1684, are typical:

> *You will forthwith sail to Petit Guavos and deliver my letter to the Governor, demanding satisfaction for a sloop of this island unlawfully seized by Captain Yankey. If the Governor justifies Yankey, you will protest against the injustice of the proceedings. If he seems to admit the illegality of the proceedings of the privateers you will consider Yankey as a pirate and tell the Governor that you will treat him as such. But if he lay the blame on the Intendant of Martinique we must carry our complaint elsewhere. If you meet with Yankey on your way you will endeavour to seize him and carry him with you to Petit Guavos. If the Governor justifies him you will deliver Yankey to him; if not, you will bring Yankey here for trial. You will demand delivery of all English subjects engaged in privateering, but not compel it by force.* [13]

These complex instructions reveal the delicacy of such tasks as entrusted to Navy personnel. Yankey, a Dutch privateer, was suspected of piracy, but if proven to be in possession of a privateer's commission from the French, he could not easily be prosecuted as a pirate. The hunters of these turbulent men had to enter into difficult negotiations, to be prepared at one moment to arrest – by force if necessary – the target of their attention, and carry him off to trial and an almost certain death, along with his crew, and at the next, to acknowledge the legitimacy of the same man's actions, and politely request the release of those English subjects who were in his service. In the event, Captain Mitchell negotiated with the French to demand the hand over of those English men who were serving in the privateer vessel La Trompeuse. However, only three of the crew were eventually recovered: "the rest were fled into the woods". [14]

Captain Solgard, stationed at New York during one of the most turbulent decades of pirate activity off the American coast, in the 1720s, may now be a forgotten name, but in his day he was warmly congratulated for his heroic defeat of the notorious Edward Low. [15]

THE PIRATE'S WEAPON OF CHOICE

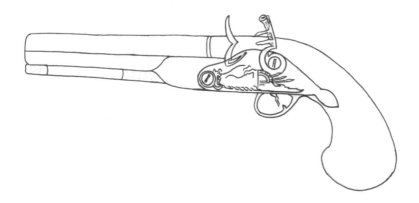

Pirates, in their heyday, were objects of dread not only to seafarers, but to settlers both in the Caribbean and on the American mainland, whose livelihoods - even their very subsistence - could be threatened by the activities of these outlaws.For generations of Caymanians, the pirate scourge was all too real. As early as 1669, when fishermen's shacks on Little Cayman were burnt in a corsair raid, and for many years afterwards, settlers were frequently threatened by marauders of many nations. However, if Cayman's links with English colonies like Jamaica made her an easy prey for nations hostile to British interests, it was also true that buccaneers and outlaws might also find a refuge on these islands. At various times in Cayman's history, groups of such individuals sought a temporary shelter or a place of permanent settlement here.

A French memorandum on the Cayman Islands, dating from around 1670, reported that "*residents of Jamaica and English buccaneers frequent the islands, as well as pirates from Ile de la Tortue and a few French merchant ships*". The report recognized English jurisdiction over Cayman noting that they *"rely on the fishing grounds to provision the buccaneers that they send out to sea, and also to supply food to a part of the population of Jamaica".* [16]

In 1667, Cayman was again involved in a pirate attack when a convoy of five ships was reportedly "taken at the Caimanos" occasioning great losses. The Duke of York was reputed to have been concerned in the venture to the tune of £3,000, while the failure to have a man of war available to escort the fleet was greatly deprecated. Again, in 1680, when a Spanish vessel captured a French ship off Grand Cayman, the captor noted that the islands were frequented by French corsairs, who had made Little Cayman their headquarters. [17] Two years later, the Captain of a French pirate ship admitted to the Spanish that pirates regularly resorted to Cayman [18]

The recognition that Cayman waters often harboured pirates, meant that patrols regularly cruised around the islands. In 1715, pirate hunter, Captain Francis Knighton, sought refuge from a storm in North Sound, Grand Cayman when his sloop, the Jamaica, ran onto the reefs and had to be abandoned. The captain was acquitted of culpability in the incident, which nevertheless revealed that pirates were not the only dangers lurking off the shores of Cayman.[19] In 1723, the Governor of Bermuda reported that a number of pirates had been captured from 'Camanos', [20] and in another incident which took place in 1737, an armed English schooner was seized by a Spanish frigate 8 leagues east of Grand Cayman. It was taken to the port of Campeche, Yucatan, but was released by a prize court in Merida. [21]

Caymanians began to be associated, deservedly or not, with piracy. A critical account of the inhabitants of Grand Cayman, sent by Spanish Captain Don Juan Tirri, was forwarded to the Governor of Cuba in 1798. Describing the island as a 'pirate's nest', he recommended that Spain should seek its destruction:

> *The islet is inhabited by a handful of lawless men who bear the name, and accidentally carry on the trade of fisher-folk, but who are in reality nothing more than sea robbers. The island constitutes their lair and it is the place where they hide their ill-gotten gains … they very*

often witness, or soon hear of the frequent shipwrecks of the mariners driven onto ... reefs. Instead of giving them assistance and help that humanity demands, they hasten thither only to rob them and take to their caves even more fragments of broken vessels. They make no exception even for English boats sailing from Jamaica many of which fall into their clutches. [22]

In 1812, Thomson's updated version of Alcedo's Geographical Dictionary, described Grand Cayman as *"inhabited by 160 people, who are descendants of the old Buccaniers ... the people are vigorous, and commonly live to a great age. They raise all kinds of produce for their own use and to spare. Their chief employment is to pilot vessels to the adjacent islands, and to fish for turtle; with which last they supply Port Royal and other places in great quantities".* [23]

Into the 19th century, the region around Cayman continued to be notable for pirate activity. In 1829, HM Schooner, Sky Jack, was patrolling the area between Grand Cayman and the south coast of Cuba *"in search of a vessel which had been taken and plundered, and the crew murdered by Pirates".* By this period, however, the men of the Royal Navy were just as likely to be looking for slave traders as for pirates: in 1839, for example, the Sappho captured a schooner carrying slaves off Grand Cayman. As late as 1922, an act of piracy was recorded, involving a Cuban and two Caymanians. [24]

WEAPONS USED IN PIRATE ATTACKS

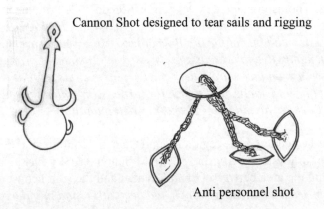

Cannon Shot designed to tear sails and rigging

Anti personnel shot

A grappling hook

VICTIMS OF PIRACY

The islanders and the scores of hapless travellers, innocent fisher folk, traders and other voyagers who were captured, tormented and terrorized by pirates, are often forgotten or glossed over in popular accounts of brigandage. Yet the depositions made by men and women who fell into the hands of pirates are among the most dramatic of documents which remain to tell the tale of those desperate times.

State sponsored piracy at times of war when wholesale pillage was the norm, had a devastating effect on local populations caught up in the carnage. Caymanian fishermen and logwood cutters, working in and around Spanish territories, were particularly vulnerable to attack by Spanish privateers.

The journal of Jonas Clough, an Englishman taken prisoner by the Spanish in 1680 on the island of Triste, survives to relate the details of what could befall those who fell into enemy hands. The group of logwood cutters, numbering around 90 persons, asked to be conveyed either to Jamaica or Cayman by their Spanish captors, but they were taken instead to Vera Cruz, packed into "a close and stinking tan house", forced to work and given very little food. They were then shackled and marched to Mexico. Here they worked for some months as artisans, before being sent to work with weavers, crowded 100 to a room, plagued with lice and forced to card 10 lbs of wool a day. One man who died was mutilated, dragged through the city and left to the dogs. Only Jonas Clough escaped – fleeing first to Havana and then obtaining a passage to Cadiz in a Portuguese ship. [25]

A SPANISH
SOLDIER

The Cayman Islanders, in their relatively small and isolated settlements, continued to be harassed by Spanish marauders well into the 19th century. An English missionary described their very real problems in a letter dated 1841:

> *The people here have suffered a great deal from the Spaniards from Cuba who appear to entertain feelings of animosity and revenge which they take every opportunity to execute. The people have been basely murdered, their vessels burnt and destroyed or taken into their ports and crews imprisoned and vessels confiscated even in times of peace and without preferring any charges against them. They have frequently applied to the Government for a redress of these repeated injuries but somehow or the other no notice has yet been taken of their application.* [26]

He also reported that in the late 1780s the Cayman Islanders had organized themselves into a militia to protect their families from Spanish invasion. Descents were most frequent at the western end of Grand Cayman. The Spaniards reportedly committed arson attacks, destroying houses and property, as well as kidnapping the inhabitants, and taking them to Cuba.

Whilst the pirate history of Cayman is now celebrated annually, the sufferings of islanders in the past, and the numberless individuals who lost their lives at the hands of such brigands, should also be part of our collective memory.

A MODERN 'PIRATE' CRUIZING OFF CAYMAN

REFERENCES

1. ADM 51/52 Log of HMS Adventure, Captain Thomas Fitzhebert, Nov. 1767-Aug 1769.
2. J. Shuter, *Exquemelin and the Pirates of the Caribbean*, p. 6, 14-15; and see C. Haring, *The Buccaneers in the West Indies in the XVII Century*.
3. CSP no 1563 Despatch of Sir Thomas Lynch.
4. N. Pickford, *The Atlas of Ship Wreck & Treasure*, p. 62-63.
5. PRO CO 1/27 Deposition of Johan Boys.
6. S. Johnson, *Sunken Ships and Treasure*, p. 370; J. Shuter, op. cit., p 16-17.
7. J. Pascall, *Pirates and Privateers*, p. 40.
8. M. Oliver, *Blackbeard and his murderous mateys*, p. 29-31.
9. J. Shuter, op. cit., p. 18-19.
10. PRO CO 37/10 Deposition of Edward North; CO 137/14 Deposition of John Shattock.
11. M. Oliver, op.cit., p 65.
12. PRO CO 1/19 Despatch from Governor of Jamaica, 20 Feb 1664.
13. CSP 1681-1685 no 1958 23 Nov 1684 Instructions from Colonel Hender Molesworth to Captain Mitchell, RN, HMS Ruby.
14. Ibid., no 2000 11Dec 1684 Captain Mitchell to Lt. Governor Molesworth.
15. CSP 1722-1723 No 606 Governor Burnet to Lord Carteret, 25 June 1723.
16. Bibliotheque Nationale de Paris, Departement des Manuscrits, Fond Colbert, vol 31, Receuil de Relations et Memoires sur l'Espagne, les Indes... [c. 1670], folios 622-623 'Des Isles Caymans'. See English translation by W.A. Hart in CINA MSD 145.
17. AGI, Escribania 47B; see also CINA MSD 120. For a discussion of the 1667 incident see CSP 1661-68 no 1537 30 July 1667 Sir Thomas Modyford to Lord Arlington; James Modyford to Lord Arlington, no 1538, 30 July 1667.
18. Confession of Captain Ubinet, 20 Feb 1682, AGI Indiferente 2578, fol 189; see also CINA MSD 172.
19. PRO ADM 1/5271 Court Martial held on board his Majesty's Ship the Shewbury in Chatham River on Monday 12 March 1715/16. For details of the incident, see ADM 51/4225 Captains Logs, Log of HMS Jamaica.
20. PRO CO 37/10 Colonel Hope, Lt Governor of Bermuda, 21 Feb 1723
21. AGI Escribania 312; see CINA MSD 120.
22. Quoted in Smith, op. cit., p. 172.
23. G.A. Thomson, *Geographical Dictionary*, London, 1812, p 347.

24. CINA MSD 174/1 HM Schooner Sky Jack, Apr. 1828-Apr. 1829, 13 Jan.
    1829; MSD 174/19 HM Sloop Sappho, 1838-9. For a brief account of
    the 1922 incident see Smith, R.S. op. cit., p. 111.
25. CSP 1681-1685 no 303 23-24 Nov. 1681 Journal and narrative of
    Jonas Clough. See also PRO CO 1/47 p. 233-43 'draft of a Memorial to
    be delivered to D.P. Ronquillo, Ambassador of Spain, touching injuries
    done the English in America'.
26. Quoted in R.S. Smith, *The Maritime Heritage of the Cayman Islands,*
    p. 67-8 .

**RECRUITS
FOR A
PRIVATEER
EXPEDITION**

H.Pyle, *The Buccaneers*, 1891

CHAPTER TWO

FROM DRAKE TO CROMWELL: PRIVATEERING EXPEDITIONS AND THE ROLE OF CAYMAN

The Cayman Islands played a crucial role in the victualling of privateering expeditions which competed to establish paramountcy in Caribbean waters from the late 16th century onwards. The location and relative isolation of Cayman were also considered advantageous for buccaneers which helped to establish the region as a favoured haunt. Although the islands came under the sphere of English influence from the mid 17th century, they were not permanently settled until much later, enabling the Spanish, Dutch and French to make continuing use of them as a source of food and water, and as a rendezvous point.

FRANCIS DRAKE'S WEST INDIAN VOYAGE, 1585-6

One of the earliest and most celebrated examples of the recourse to the Cayman Islands by privateers is found in accounts of the West Indian voyage of the man described as Queen Elizabeth's 'favourite pirate' - Francis Drake. He set out on this privateering expedition from Plymouth on 14th September 1585, with a fleet of around 25 vessels, including two royal ships and several pinnaces. Among the larger of the ships was the 'Primrose', of 300-400 tons, captained by Martin Frobisher, vice admiral of the fleet and a distinguished explorer and naval officer. A prime objective of the fleet was to harass Spanish possessions, and hopefully capture some rich prizes.

After sailing to Spain, and then to the Canaries, where the fleet failed to land, and on to the Cape Verde islands, a course was set for the West Indies. An epidemic of fever en route resulted in many deaths, and Christmas was spent on St Christopher's for recuperation. An attack was mounted on the Spanish island of Hispaniola, and on leaving the island at the end of January, the fleet made for Cartagena, another significant Spanish stronghold, where they secured large sums in ransom money from the inhabitants. Moving out in mid April, Drake's men sailed toward Cuba. After touching briefly at the Cayman islands, they stopped at Cape San Antonio in western Cuba for water and firewood. Towards the end of May they attacked the Spanish settlement of St Augustine, finally returning to Portsmouth towards the end of July 1586.

Drake's raids on Spanish Santo Domingo and Carthagena caused rejoicing, but it had already begun to dawn on the financial backers that the expedition had not captured the breathtaking prizes hoped for; in fact had made only modest financial returns, while many men had been lost. The voyage nevertheless served as the opening action in a naval war between England and Spain, which was to have further

repercussions in the Caribbean. [1]

FRANCIS DRAKE

(The World Encompassed, 1628)

Various narratives of the voyage survive, which have provided us with a number of versions of the stop-over at Cayman. The so-called Map Text – a calendar of major events provided as a text to accompany the general map of the voyage – notes as follows:

> *The 20. of Aprill we fell with two Ilands called Caimanes, vhere we refreshed our selves with many Allagartas and greate Turoises, being very ugly and fearefull beasts to behold, but were made good meate to eate, and so the next day we departed thence towards Cape Saint Antony.*[2]

The two islands were Grand and Little Cayman, and as the narrator reveals, the privateers made good use of the live food sources found there. A newsletter of the voyage provides further details of this stop-over, indicating that the landing was effected on Grand Cayman, and revealing that as well as 'alligators' and turtles, the mariners also helped themselves to 'coneys', a type of West Indian shellfish:

> *The 20 of Apryll we Landed our men at Cuny Grand [and] tooke plenty of turtles, Alygathaes, Coneys, etc. The 23 we set sayle agayne.*[3]

The Primrose Journal, possibly written by Henley, was a record of events aboard the vice admiral's ship, and recorded the visit to Cayman somewhat more picturesquely:

> *wee fell with an Ile that had no people in hit. There wee fownde strawnge kindes of beastes & killed more than xx Alligatos. Those bee suche serpents as have bin in London to be seene. There weare Crocadiles which did Incounter & fighte with us, they live bothe in the sea & on lande. Wee tooke divers & made verie good meate of them; some of the same were ten foote in lengthe. Also wee killed other little beastes like cattes & other little serpents abowte 2 foote longe called Guanos, with a great number of Turtles of huge bignes which served us for verie good meat;*
> *This Ilande is a verie Deserte & wildernesse & so full of woodes as hit can growe. Wee thought to have watered there but could finde none. Wee staid there ij Daies & set the woodes on fire & soe departed.*[4]

The narrator's description of the crocodiles, turtles and iguanas encountered is a useful early description of Cayman's fauna, and it is a revelation to learn that the privateers took on and fought with the alligators they found there, and consumed their flesh with gusto.

Indeed, manuscripts of the Drake voyage are peppered with drawings of the exotic creatures met with on the journey, together with details of their appearance and habits.

THE 'ALLIGATOR' OF CAYMAN

A strange beast drawne after the life, & is called by our English mariners Aligarta, by the Spaniards Caiman, which liveth both at sea and land, he watcheth the Tortoise when she laieth egges, & when the Tortoise is done from them he will hunt them out, & devour them all that he findeth. He hath bene seene by the Spaniards to take hold of an oxe or cow by the taile and so to draw them forcibly into the sea, and there devour them: & so likewise a man whom he hath surprised asleepe or otherwise at unwares: for if he be in time espied a man may well escape by flight, for he runeth not so fast as a man, but with pieces & pikes we killed many in desolate Islands and eate them, whose flesh is most like to veale in sight, but the olde are somewhat rammish in taste: the young of half growth are very speciall good meate, his back is well armed with a strong scale, but his belly soft, and between the forlegge and the body is the best place to strike him with a pike, they are of eight or nine foot long and some lesse, his backe of a darkish gray colour, his belly whitish yellow.

(Bigges, *Drake's West Indian Voyage*, 1589).

THE CAYMAN SEA TURTLE

A Tortoise is a fish that liveth in the sea but cometh to the land to lay his egges in breeding time, and goung upon her finnes which are strong and tough, commeth to the sand some 40 or 50 pases from the sea, there with her fore finnes scrapeth a hole in the sand, and so turning her hinder parte in the said hole laieth her egge, which at one time are about one hundred, and so scraping the sand over the egges againe to hide them, goeth her way to the sea and never commeth againe, the egges by the heat of the sunne are in due time hatched, and the yong go presently to the sea one following of an other, with whom if the Aligarta doe meet, he devoureth the one after an other as they come. This Tortoises flesh is good meate, & is like unto beefe both in tast and shew, the egges are also very good saving that they have a little rammish tast (as to me seemeth) but many others liked them wel, the scale of the backe which is but one shell is about 3 foot long, and 2 foote and a halfe broad, whereof many are used for targets against arrowes, or any other edged weapon. In the Islands of Caimanes we killed a hundred in two nights, where we killed also many Aligartas aforesaid, & therwith refreshed our people greatly. The Tortoise in the night comming up to lay egges as is aforeaid, is watched by us, who purposely walking along by the sea side, as soone as we can espie them on land either going up or comming downe, we runne to take holde of them, who runneth but slowly, and so overturne them by the side of the backe shell, and lay them on their backs, and so leaving them go on to seeke more until the morning, and then gather them all together, for they cannot possibly turne themselves on their belly againe. [5]

(Bigges, *Drake's West Indian Voyage*, 1589).

It is interesting to note that the privateers could find no source of fresh water. This was a complaint to be repeated by other visitors around this time and may help to explain why Cayman was not targeted for more systematic settlement at this period.

THE PRIVATEERING VOYAGE OF WILLIAM KING, 1592

Captain King set sail from Ratcliffe on 26 January 1592. The 200 ton 'Salomon' carrying 100 mariners and the 40 ton Jane Bonaventure, with a crew of 26, were on a voyage to the bay of Mexico. The privateers carried a commission which had been granted to a group of London merchants:

to sett out to the seas the Gartrude, the Salomon, and two small pinnaces in warlike sorte against the Kinge of Spayne, and his Subjectes in any of his dominions for recovery of goodes deteyned by him and them under such articles and conditions which are sett downe by the Lords of the Privy Counsell and agreed upon on that behalfe.

EXTRACT OF AN ENGLISH PRIVATEERING COMMISSION AGAINST THE KING OF SPAIN'S SHIPS

The fleet sailed past Kent and on to Portugal, and from thence to Lanzarote in the Canary Islands where several men were landed and a brass cannon seized from the inhabitants. Three of the Canary Islanders were killed in the melee. At Grand Canaria they were also fired on while attempting to board a barque anchored there.

King then directed a course for the West Indies, and the privateers reached Dominica around 10th April. Here they seized a 100 ton Guineaman laden with 270 slaves. At San Juan de Puerto Rico they seized two further prizes, one with a cargo of Canary wines. Most of the negroes were landed, and the prize laden with wine, was sent home, while the other was set on fire. After watering at the isle of Mona and taking on potatoes and plantains, they sailed on to Santo Domingo, where a 15 ton boat carrying molasses was seized. The privateers then shaped a course towards the south coast of Jamaica, stopping off at Cayman on the way. As King's narrative stated:

We ranged the three islands of the Caimanes, and landed at Grand Caiman, being the Westernmost, where we found no people, but a good river of fresh water; and there we turned up threescore great tortoises; and of them we tooke our choise, to wit, fifteene of the females, which are the best and fullest of egges, whereof two served an hundred men a day. And there with stones we might kill turtle doves, wilde geese, & other good fowles at our pleasure.

From Cayman the privateers continued on to Cuba and to the Tortugas. At Rio de Puercos, on the Cuban coast, a 20 ton barque was seized. This carried live pigs, dried pork and ox hides. A few days later, another ship, of 80 tons, carrying hides, indigo and spices was taken, and a 20 ton frigate, with a cargo of linen, shortly thereafter. One of the Spanish prizes was brought home by quartermaster Richard Southey, who recounted the skirmish in a deposition made before the High Court of Admiralty which adjudicated in such matters:

beyond the Avana nere the Isle of Cuba they mett with a Spanishe shippe of aboute L. tonnes whereunto this examinate & company gave chase all the day and in the evening comminge nere the shore all the company in the said shipp tooke them into the boate & forsoke the shippe, soe as this examinate and company comminge on borde founde she was laden with hides noe livinge person beinge lefte on borde, which the Captaine & master caused to be manned & sent for England.

By May, off Havana, two more boats laden with tortoises had been taken and sunk, and the men aboard them set on shore. A number of skirmishes with Spanish ships followed, and the taking of further prizes with cargoes of wine, oil, hides and chests of gold. The ship carrying gold was also taken home as a prize, commanded by Laurence Cocke. King finally set sail for England and arrived at Dover around 10 November 1592. [6]

TURNING TURTLES

(P. Labat, *Nouveau Voyage aux Iles*, 1727).

DUTCH PRIVATEERS AND THE WRECK OF THE 'DOLFIJN' ON GRAND CAYMAN, 1631

The English were not the only seafaring nation in quest of Spanish treasure ships. Dutch privateers also made frequent sorties to the Caribbean. The journal of Everts Sybrants van Staveren reported arriving at the 'middle Cayman' in March 1612, and sending some of his people on land "*to examine the island and to see if anything good can be found … but because of the multitude of caymans or crocodiles which were on the beach and came shooting out of the water and were terrible to see they were worried to be bitten … these two islands … are empty in the interior and swampy and full of caymans and crocodiles which live in the woods*". [7]

A DUTCH PRIVATEER CAPTAIN

In 1624 at least two Dutch ships touched at Cayman where they reported the usual sightings of 'alligators' and feasted on turtle meat. One of the ships' logs remarked that Grand Cayman was "bad, empty country with a dirty coastline in the east". They anchored on the west side of the island "in a large sandy bay, in 12 and 13 fathoms of water". [8] In 1626 a Dutch fleet evidently used Cayman as a rendezvous point during manoeuvres with ships of hostile nations. The fleet was ordered to disperse "better to observe the enemy's ships and to converge again around the Cayman Islands". The following year, another rendezvous was made around Little Cayman where the fleet stopped overnight to obtain turtle, this being the season when they came ashore to lay their eggs. [9]

In 1629 a squadron of ships was sent out by the Dutch West India Company under the command of Admiral Pater. In total, eleven ships, carrying 842 sailors, 326 soldiers and more than 500 cannon set sail. Meanwhile, another Dutch fleet commanded by Admiral Pieter Adriaensz, also cruising the Caribbean, stopped at the Cayman Islands around 1630 describing them as:

> *two empty small islands, so they cannot be seen from more than 4 or 5 miles distance. The easternmost one is very steep on the eastern end, with a cliff-like tip, and the side very beautiful without dirt; stretches WSW about 3 miles long. The western end is an empty Point, behind which one can lay at anchor in 6, 7 and 10 fathoms of water, so that one can easily lose a cable and anchor. The second is about 2 miles NNW from there, and is shaped like a triangle. ... very tasty turtles come and lay their eggs in the sand from May until October ... so that in one night one can obtain one or two thousand ... Here a lot of caymans show themselves, after which these islands were named; there are also many sea birds, good to eat. Otherwise the islands are very dry, rocky and sandy, without fresh water and fruits.*

Admiral Pater's fleet was crossing from Colombia to Cuba when Captain Joachim Gijsen's ship, the 'Dolfijn', became separated from the other ships. The 'Dolfijn', badly rigged, dropped below Jamaica, and was eventually wrecked on Grand Cayman. The loss was attributed to "poor supervision by the helmsmen". For four long months, the captain and a crew, numbering around 122 men and boys, were marooned there. During their enforced stay, they salvaged some artillery and planks from their wrecked ship, and constructed a yacht which they called the 'Cayman'. Hiding some of the armaments they recovered on the island, they embarked several pieces on the yacht, and set out for the American mainland, hoping to find the rest of the fleet. Admiral Pater had already left for home, but the survivors from the 'Dolfijn' met up with the fleet of Pieter Adrieansz who advised them to abandon the 'Cayman' yacht, and dispersed them over his own ships. [10]

THE PRIVATEERING VOYAGE OF WILLIAM JACKSON, 1642

The English Puritans had always been interested in colonisation and in 1629 a company headed by the Earl of Warwick had founded a colony on an uninhabited island off the coast of Nicaragua called Santa Catalina, later referred to as Old Providence. It became a haven for privateers. The Spanish, concerned at this encroachment, sent an expedition against it in 1641 which led to the deportation of the colonists with the women and children sent back to England and the men, numbering around 770, taken as prisoners to Spain. [11]

In retaliation, the following year, an expedition headed by Captain William Jackson sailed for the West Indies in three men-of-war with letters of reprisal from the Earl of Warwick. He signed on more than a thousand men in the Caribbean. They were mostly from St Kitts and Barbados, perhaps discharged mariners, or ex-indentured servants. Jackson and his Vice Admiral were both 'old Providence hands', and no doubt well known to the habitual seafarers and opportunists who hung out in Caribbean ports. [12]

The recruits were all hoping for rich prizes from a planned cruise along the Spanish Main from Venezuela to Honduras. Sailing west from Jamaica, the privateers touched at Cayman which Jackson described as follows:

> *This place is low land & all rockye, & there bee two Islands of ye same name & Quallitie, being by ye Spanyards called Chimanos, from ye multitude of Alligators here found which are Serpents, if not resembling ye Crocodiles of Egypt. Hither doe infinitt numbers of Sea Tortoises yearly resorte to lay their Eggs upon ye Sandy Bay, which at this time swarmed so thicke. The Island is much frequented by English, Dutch & French ships, that come purposely to salt up ye flesh of these Tortoises.* [13]

Jackson's privateers attacked the port of La Guaira in Caracas in December 1642, but were repulsed by the Spanish. Undeterred, Jackson went on to bombard Maiquetia and Puerto Cabello before taking the city of Maracaibo in December, remaining in occupation until early 1643. By now commanding an 11 vessel squadron, Jackson stopped off at Jamaica, landing 500 men, but, sparing the Spanish capital in exchange for a small ransom, the privateers turned for home. England could now lay claim to being a "major Caribbean player". [14]

OLIVER CROMWELL

(Taylor, *The Western Design*, 1965)

THE CROMWELL EXPEDITION, 1654-59

This expeditionary force, sent out on a grand design against Spanish possessions, ultimately had to content itself with the relatively small prize of Jamaica. But it set in train an English influence over the region which had profound consequences for the future of the Cayman Islands.

In April 1654 the first Dutch War had ended and Cromwell decided that an attack on Spanish possessions in the Indies would be both popular and profitable. Secret preparations for the expedition were assisted by Thomas Gage who had great experience of the West Indies as a Dominican priest, and by Thomas Modyford, a barrister and Barbados planter. Volunteers were sought from English regiments, but in practice officers used the exercise to rid themselves of undesirable characters with the result that the recruits were described as *"cheats, thieves, cutpurses, and such like lewd persons, who had long time lived by sleight of hand, and dexterity of wit"*. [15]

Five regiments were formed, the first headed by General Venables, with Edward D'Oyley as his Lieutenant Colonel. The latter was a 37 year old officer who had served in Wiltshire and Ireland. Overall command was given to Admiral Penn and General Venables, and the expedition was billed as the first stage of a grandiose plan of conquest which became known as the 'Western Design'.

Arriving in Barbados on 29 January Venables managed to recruit a large additional force by dint of proclaiming that any bond-servants who volunteered would have their freedom. Many planters lost a large part of their labour force by these means. Freemen, escaping debts, also joined up. In all, 3-4,000 men were enlisted. The island was also stripped of pikes and matchlocks, powder and ball to arm the troops. The 'Marston Moor' and the 'Selby' had meanwhile been dispatched to St Christopher (then shared by the English and the French) and had enlisted 800 there, 300 in Nevis and 80 in Montserrat. The expedition now commanded over 8,000 landforces.

However, after landing at Hispaniola, and following several skirmishes with the cattle hunters, or buccaneers, the offensive failed. Rain made conditions miserable and dysentery decimated the troops. By 4th May, more than a 1,000 men had been lost and the expedition re-embarked, humiliated and defeated. [16]

So as not to return to England empty handed, it was decided to attack Jamaica - an easier prize. Under Spanish hands, the island did not have a population of more than 2,500. The expedition landed on Jamaica on 10 May 1655, and met little resistance on its way to the town of Villa de la Vega (St Jago), occupying it the next day. On the 16th the Spanish Governor agreed to terms of capitulation.

Within weeks of the landing on Jamaica, supplies were running low for the numerous troops, which that island's scant resources could not easily supply. The soldiers made several abortive attempts to cultivate crops, but dysentery and malaria were claiming more than a hundred lives a week. Cayman now proved crucial to the victualling of the men as Penn sent 3 ships – the 'Arms of Holland', 'Falmouth' and 'Dove' to the islands to catch turtles. They obtained a good supply from the French ships which habitually gathered there for the season. They were soon sent back for more, but found the French ships gone. [17]

Reinforcements arrived with Robert Sedgwick on 1 October 1655, whose fleet of 11 ships brought stores and a regiment of 800 men. The sight that greeted him, he described as "sad and deplorable". Many of the men had been reduced to eating rats, snakes and lizards. The shallow graves of English soldiers had been dug up by Spanish dogs, and the bodies eaten. By November 1655 only 3,710 men remained of the 7,000 landed in May. A stench of death hung over the town. [18]

Cromwell ordered the dispatch of 2 more regiments, and provisions for 6,000 men, but in April 1656 rations were again low and men began to desert. By July, supplies were being obtained from private turtlers which arrived from Cayman, and the need to conserve food led General d'Oyley to issue a general order about waste prevention and to decrease rations in the following month from a weekly supply of 15 lbs of turtle and the same of flour, to 1 lb of turtle, 12 lbs of flour and a half gallon of peas. By October, there was no more turtle, and the men were being given 12 lbs of flour and 3 quarts of oatmeal. Over the following years, seasonal supplies of turtle were procured, but in 1659, d'Oyley was reporting that he had been obliged to send home the Marston Moor, which had exhausted its victuals and was in a state of some turbulence. [19]

In April 1661, d'Oyley further informed the Commissioners of the Admiralty at Whitehall that he:

Was forced, for want of provisions, to send the ship Bear home, for if he should not take hold of the season of killing turtle at Kiemanas, he must have been forced to have laid her up, and by what extraordinary courses he has maintained her all this time, the steward general will inform them.

The seasonal taking of turtle at Cayman had now become an annual necessity and with the regular visits of turtlers, small settlements on the islands developed. It is believed, indeed that among the first inhabitants of Cayman, were deserters from Cromwell's famished army. Meanwhile, Admiral Penn, who had left Jamaica on 25 June 1655, was considered to have prematurely deserted his post, and on arriving home, was arrested and sent to the Tower. Venables, who had also sailed for home - on the 4th of July - was consigned to the same fate. Both were released after a few weeks in captivity.

Jamaica, however, was beginning the process of conversion into an English colony. Would-be colonists were rounded up between 1656 and 1658 and these began arriving on the island. Quakers and Bermudians were among them. A fort was commissioned which was to be the beginning of the settlement that was to become Port Royal. In 1657 d'Oyley encouraged the buccaneers living on Tortuga to bring their prizes to Port Royal. This gave a further fillip to the town.

The development of Jamaica's Port Royal as a haven of privateers, and the role of Cayman as a satellite of the English settlement, was to have important consequences for future actions in the region.

REFERENCES

1. M. Keeler, *Sir Francis Drake's West Indian Voyage 1585-86*, passim.
2. ibid., the Map Text, p 68.
3. ibid., p. 113 A Newsletter [British Library Cotton MS Otho E VIII, fols 235-236v].
4. ibid., p. 202-3 The Primrose Journal [BL Royal MS 7 C xvi fols 166-73].
5. W. Bigges, *Sir Francis Drake's West Indian Voyage*, p28.
6. K. R. Andrews. (ed) *English Privateering Voyages to the West Indies, 1588-95*, p. 213-16, 391.
7. CINA MSD 286 Copy of extracts from the Journal of Everts Sybrants van Staveren on the Voyage to the West Indies, 1611-1612, Dutch National Archives
8. J. De Laet, *History of the West India Company*, 1931-7 edn., vol. 1 p. 42 and p 125, [and see translations from the original Dutch by J. Liebaers in CINA MSD 284].
9. ibid., p. 137-8; vol 2 p. 27.
10. ibid., p 169-173 and see R.S. Smith, op. cit., p. 151.
11. J.S. Bromley, *Corsairs and Navies, 1660-1760*, p. 8.
12. S.A.G. Taylor, *The Western Design. An Account of Cromwell's Expedition to the Caribbean*, p. 4.
13. W. Jackson, 'Brief Journal', 24, quoted in R.S. Smith, op cit., p. 87.
14. D.F. Marley, *Pirates: Adventurers of the High Seas*, p 21-24.
15. S.A.G. Taylor, op. cit., p. xi, 2, 5.
16. ibid., p. 10, 15, 18, 29, 31, 36.
17. CSP 1675-76 no 218 Vice Admiral William Goodson, to the Commissioners of the Admiralty and Navy, 24 July 1655.
18. S.A.G. Taylor, op. cit., p. 90
19. CSP 1675-76, no 318 June 7 1659, D'Oyley to Commissioners. See also R.S. Smith, op.cit, p. 61-62.

CHAPTER THREE

PIRATE AND PRIVATEER ACTIONS IN AND AROUND CAYMAN

While the Cayman Islands took on an important role in provisioning privateers, they increasingly also played host to communities of corsairs, buccaneers and others . Their reputation as a haunt and a lair for renegades, inevitably meant that attacks on shipping and on the settlers themselves began to occur in and around Cayman. A new phase in the islands' pirate history was unfolding.

A FRENCH BUCCANEER COMMUNITY MAROONED ON CAYMAN, 1653-4

The small island of Tortuga, off Hispaniola, had long been a haunt of buccaneers of various nations. At different times under French and English control, the Spanish launched numerous attacks against this irritant, so close to their own territories. In 1640, a French Huguenot named Levasseur established a foothold on Tortuga. Under his command, the small colony prospered, but his increasing despotism exasperated the inhabitants, and he was finally murdered by two of his own protégés – Captains Martin and Tibaud - in 1653. A new Governor was appointed, the Chevalier de Fontenay, who arrived with his brother.

In November of that year, however, a Spanish expedition of five vessels and 400 infantry was sent against the French settlement on Tortuga, which had an active population of around 700. The French capitulated and the inhabitants were given three days to prepare two ships for sea to carry them away. During this time, Monsieur Hotman, the Governor's brother, was taken hostage by the Spanish. Half of the inhabitants were placed in one vessel with Martin and Tibaut, and the rest went in the other boat with the Governor and his brother.

What happened next is unclear, but in the version of the story told by Du Tertre as recorded in his Caribbean history published between 1667 and 1671, Martin and Tibaut separated the healthy and strong men from those who were weak and ailing, and together with the women, offloaded the latter in the Cayman Islands. According to Du Tertre, the women and the sick men were left at the mercy of the island's crocodiles, whilst the brothers regained their boat, which had, however, suffered considerable damage, having lost its sail, cables and ammunition. Deciding to await better luck, they were careening the

vessel when a passing Dutch ship, seeing their plight, offered to provide them with the necessary supplies to enable them to return to France. What became of the group abandoned on Cayman is not known. [1]

A FRENCH BUCCANEER

(Exquemelin, *Boucaniers of America*, 1684)

A PORTUGUESE PRIVATEER AT CAYMAN, 1664

Privateering was an activity which whilst in theory authorising
ship's captains to seize hostile vessels as a patriotic duty, in
practice permitted rogues of many nationalities to prey on
merchant shipping in the name of countries, with which they
might themselves have only a tenuous connection. The activities
of Captain John Douglas in 1664, off Cayman, reveal both the
unscrupulous character of such 'privateers', and the use of the
lesser islands as a lair for pirates, while stalking their quarry.

Douglas obtained his warrant as a privateer in 1662. On 10th
September of that year a Portuguese Commission was accorded to
Charles de Bils. He in turn, gave the letter of marque to a man
named John Douglas, constituting him, on 20 September 1662,
*"Commander of my shipp called St John in my name and as if I
were personally present to make warr with the enimies of this
crowne of Portugall".* [2]

Armed with this, Douglas set sail, and we next meet him in 1664,
anchored off Cayman Brac, lying in wait for a ship called the 'Blue
Dove'. The testimony of Daniel Sprague, a sailor who boarded
Douglas' ship at the Brac, demonstrates how an ordinary mariner
could become caught up in acts of piracy:

> *when I wasse Cleerr and my wages paid me I could get noe
> imployment nor passage, ... to goe to the windword Ilands. Then I
> thought good to goe as to Cammanus, to see if I could get passage
> there, and I saild with one Captaine Hermon towards the Cam-
> manus, and as wee Came to an iland called Camman-bricke, their
> lay Captaine John Duglasse at Anker. He sent his boate abord of us
> to heer what newse from Jemecoe, and we asked of them wether
> they weare bound. The quarter Maistor answered and said, wee be
> bound to the windword Ilands. I asked of them weither I could have
> passage with them or noe, and hee said, "Aye, and wellcome".
> Then I went abord with my Chest and Clothes and I staid aboard all
> the night and Could not speake with the Captaine, but the nixt
> Mornin as soon as it wasse day I spoke with the Captaine. I desired
> of the Captaine whether he wasse bound and he told me he wasse
> looking out for a shipe that came from Amsterdam in Holland to*

*Jemecoe, called the Blew Dove, and said "if I could meet with her
she is a good prise for me. I have been ten or twelve dayes aseeking
after her and Cannot light of her, but if I can light of her she is a
prise for me. I have the king of Portugalls Commishon". I, Danell
Sprage, [said] unto Captaine John Duglasse, "without your
Commishon be very firme and that you be sure you can make a
prise of her I desire you not to come neer her, for I know what the
ship is and came out of Holland in her". He answered and said if I
would goe a long with him he would beare me out in all dammages
that shuld follow or insue upon me Conserning takeing of the prise.
Then the shipe which I came from Jemecoe in wasse gon from the
Iland over to the Cammanus and their wasse noe other shipe left
but only Captaine John Duglase. I said unto Captaine John
Duglasse, "shuld I goe with you, and you shuld come up with this
shipe and take her, and the Company seeing of me they will say that
I have been at the Cammanus and have fetched a shipe on purpose
to make a prise of them". Captaine Duglasse answered and said
that "I and my Company can testifie too the contrarie and as far as
my Commishon and my life doth goe I will beare you out Against all
them that shall queshton you as Conserning the takeing of this
shipe: I am Captaine and I have taken her with my Commishon and
I will Answer it".* [3]

Thus it was that Daniel Sprague boarded the 'St. John' and then
found out that Captain Douglas was hoping to take the 'Blue Dove'
from Holland as a prize – a ship on which Sprague himself had
voyaged. The hapless mariner next provided a list of other crew
members aboard Douglas' ship who could testify that they had
already been in pursuit of the 'Blue Dove' before Sprague had
joined them. To the names of two Englishmen – William Gibbons
and John Hill—were added that of 'Cline the Dutchman, Halligert
Younson, and the Quartermaster of the 'St. John', Solomon
Begensous. Sprague also produced two witnesses *"wich can
justifie that I did desire the Captain that, without his Comishon
were sure, not to medle with the ship".*

The privateer with the Portuguese commission then set sail for
Jamaica, and anchored in Bluefields Bay, presumably aware that
homeward bound ships would stop there. Meanwhile, its quarry,

the 'Blue Dove', had sailed from Port Royal with a crew of 10 and also made for Bluefields Bay to take on water and some ballast. Whilst they were at anchor, according to John Hunter, a sailor aboard the 'Blue Dove',

Duglas came rowing upp with two oars about 8 of the clock at night. Wee hailed them and asked whence thay were and thayer answer was, from the Barbados. Wee asked who was there they answered Peter Prier, who said thay had lost Camanos and were going to seek for it againe, but presently thay clapt thayer helme a starbord and shered abord us.

Taking up the story, William Browne, a teenager who had taken a passage in the 'Blue Dove', to travel to England, reported that Douglas' men

gave them a voly of shot, being in number about 27 men, and being somewhat darke the master was shot in the arme and the men of the Blow Dove were put in the howll of the ship; and then the asaylants cut the cables and carryd away both vesells and them, until they came to Poynt Niggereell, where they met with ane English barke coming from Caymans and bownd for Porte Royall in Jamaica where they putt the said master of the Blowe Dove aboard according to his desire and furnished them with some victwales and a caise of spirits; and after they were gone owt of sight they lasht there barke aboard of the prise and took most of there things owt of her and let her goe adrifte. [4]

Charles, Hadsall, Commander of the ship 'Lucretia', which had accompanied the 'Blue Dove' from Port Royal found out later that Douglas' men had visited his own ship prior to the attack to enquire whether the 'Lucretia' would "ingage to defend the ship Blue Dove". A second group of men in a canoe had engaged the captain in conversation, pretending to make arrangements with him to sail together to Grand Cayman, when the attack on the 'Blue Dove' had taken place.

Three days afterwards, while still in Bluefields Bay, Hadsall saw a small vessel put into the bay. Boarding her, he found the wounded master of the 'Blue Dove', Robert Cook. Cook informed him that

Douglas and his men had taken everything except the clothes he wore, including valuable jewellery, chests of silver and the cargo of sugar which had been carried by the 'Blue Dove'.

Hadsall, Sprague and the others made these depositions in July 1664, and by the 16th of that month, a commission had already been given to James Oliver (a merchant in Boston) and to Edward Hutchinson to seize Douglas' ship which was known to have arrived at Piscatage. When Douglas asked for permission to water and buy victuals he was taken prisoner. Unbowed, Douglas petitioned the Boston court in August 1664 to come to a speedy decision as to whether his prize was lawful, complaining that his sailors "having been there 2 weeks were without food". He also entered a plea, arguing that the 'Blue Dove' had been "looden by the Jues under the King of Spaine" and that prisoners on board deposed that the ship belonged to Amsterdam and was bound for that port. The court ordered a monetary payment to be given to Douglas and his men to enable them to eat until they could find work, but declared the capture illegal. [5]

MUTINY OFF CAYMAN: EDWARD MORGAN'S PRIVATEERS, 1665

In June 1664, Sir Thomas Modyford landed in Jamaica as Governor. Finding the colony swarming with outlaws, he initially dealt severely with the privateers, "imprisoning their persons, condemning them of piracy, and executing some" but discovered the error of his ways within a few months, having "*found how powerfull an enemy I had [by my severe proceedings] made of those who were formerly the best friends to this place, and sadly considering what mischeife such men might bring on us, who not only knew all our portes, bayes, and creekes, but every path and highway in the Island*". Reflecting that if enough of the Jamaica based privateers joined with the French at Tortuga and Hispaniola, as some had already done, they would be well placed to attack the colony, he took advantage of the declaration of war with the Dutch, news of which reached him by Lord Arlington's dispatch of the 12th November 1664, and rumours of the likelihood of renewed hostilities with the French, to

> *change my behaviour towards these people so effectually, that I persuaded all that were in, or neare this harbour to undertake against the Dutch at Qurazao, and gave them suitable commissions, and encouragement, giving them Colonel Edward Morgan my Deputy Governor for the Generall on which they went very cheerfully without putting the King to one penny charge.* [6]

In mid April 1665, accordingly, Edward Morgan left Jamaica with a force of between 500 and 700 privateers. His commission from Sir Thomas Modyford was to "reduce the Dutch colonies". The plan was to attack the Dutch on St Christopher, from there to go to Eustacia, an island three leagues further, where the Dutch had a settlement, and to continue on to Curacao. On the homeward voyage, Morgan's men intended to "visit the French and English Buckaneers on Hispaniola and at Tortugas".

Morgan himself did not survive the expedition – he died on Eustacia – but the Dutch were routed, and the booty taken was divided amongst the men. However, as Modyford later reported, *"on the death of Colonel Morgan they scattered, and left the rest of that service unperformed, and got together again on the South Keyes of Cuba. I sent Major Beeston to treate with them for a second voyage which they promised to undertake...".* [7]

Modyford granted further commissions in March 1665, defending his actions with the comment that while the ordinary privateers spent their profits in *"armes, cloathes and drink ... some of the officers and civiller sort have setled, and are settling plantations, the owners of their shipp spend their shares in refitting"*. In November, another rendezvous of the scattered troops was organised, at which it was decided to attack Curacao. By March 1666, Modyford was reporting hopefully that the privateers had chosen Captain Edward Mansfield for their Admiral and had sailed in the middle of January from the South Keys of Cuba for Curacao.

A few weeks later he was obliged to write that lack of discipline having prevented this attack, the privateers had descended upon the island of Providence instead.

Colonel Theodore Cary, who took charge after Morgan's death, and helped plan the abortive attack on Curacao, has left a narrative of the expedition which reveals that a mutiny nearly placed the whole enterprise in jeopardy, soon after it began in April 1665:

> *wee sett saile from Port Royall, and remain'd in Blewfields bay 4 days to wood and water, which having done made for ye Caymans to furnish our selves with provisions, it being turtleing season, where lay untill ye 16th of May; here we mett with Capt Harman and ye Pearle frigott, which the Lt Generall order'd to accompany him to ye Ile of Pinos, being ye place appoynted for our rendevous, but ere wee departed from ye Caymans, most of the seamen and souldiers declared against ye conditions on which we are to proceed, refused all commands, mutined and would not sett forward, until ye Lt Generall declared his power by reading his Commission, promising that his power, and commande, should not any way take from ym any part of ye plunder, they all crying out, that great commands and many commands would take from them all ye profitt, wherupon I gave ym my word, and promise also, that I would not take from ym, any of ye booty should be gott, this with a promise likewise that all plunder should be equally divided; obeyed, and on ye 16th of May sett sail for ye Ile of Pines, where wee all met.* [8]

The mutiny off Cayman and the subsequent disorder of the troops was characteristic of such ventures. But if the corpulent Edward Morgan, who probably suffered a heart attack having "pursued over-earnestly the enemy on a hot day" did not cover himself in glory on this occasion, his nephew Henry Morgan was soon to restore the family's standing as his attacks on the Spanish Main rapidly became the talk of the day.

HENRY MORGAN'S PRIVATEERS

Having arrived in Jamaica in the 1650s, perhaps with Cromwell's army, Henry Morgan had become a captain in the Port Royal Volunteer Regiment by 1662. With his uncle serving there as Deputy Governor, Henry was bound to prosper. In 1666 he became a Colonel, and upon the death of Edward Mansfield was appointed buccaneer leader, in a clever attempt by the Governor to confer the post on a loyal officer. This was a period of renewed anti-Spanish fears, and Morgan rapidly gathered together a not inconsiderable flock of rovers, emboldened by letters of marque issued by the English governors to would-be raiders of Spanish galleons.

HENRY MORGAN

A smug and corpulent image of the man after his buccaneering days were over and he had settled into life as a prosperous and respected colonist on Jamaica.

In March 1668 Morgan led a raid on the town of Puerto Principe (present day Camaguey) in Cuba. In the same year Morgan also attacked Portobello in Panama which was defended by 3 castles. The plunder of the city, after its soldiers surrendered, involved the torture of numerous wealthy citizens, and other excesses. The treasure captured nevertheless made Morgan the most successful buccaneer in the Caribbean. Morgan went on to plunder Maracaibo (in modern Venezuela) again using torture to extract booty - he used a makeshift rack amongst other methods. [9]

PRIVATEERS ATTACKING PUERTO DE PRINCIPE

(Exquemelin, *Boucaniers of America*, 1684)

Finally, Morgan assembled 36 ships, with 2,000 men, for his greatest raid - on Panama City. On the way he captured fortresses on Santa Catalina Island. He then took Chagres in Panama before heading overland for Panama City, which he sacked.

On his return to Jamaica, the governing council passed a vote of thanks. However, England and Spain had already signed a treaty ending the war, and the Spanish protests to Charles II of England led to Morgan being shipped to England to stand trial. The Governor of Jamaica, obliged to reprove Morgan, who had a commission to attack ships, but not Spanish towns, nevertheless declared him "an honest brave fellow" while admitting "that the privateers did divers barbarous acts, which they lay to his Vice Admiral's charge". The Governor also declared himself certain that the Spanish had been planning to attack Jamaica and considered it *"very unequal that we should in any measure be restrained, while they are at liberty to act as they please upon us".*

Morgan and his officers, for their part, defended their campaigns as a spirited defence of imprisoned Englishmen. Having heard that men were kept in the dungeons at Portobello castle, for example, "they thought it their duty to attempt that place". Sent home confined in the 'Welcome' frigate, Admiral Henry Morgan carried a letter which described him as *'a very well deserving person, and one of great courage and conduct, who may, with his Majesty's pleasure, perform good public service at home or be very advantageous to this island if war should again break forth with the Spaniard'.* [10]

The hero's welcome accorded to Henry Morgan on his arrival in England led King Charles – after a suitable period - to confer a knighthood upon him, and his vindication was made complete by his appointment as Deputy Governor of Jamaica, which ironically gave him the task of suppressing buccaneers. When Morgan died – reputedly of the effects of drink - in 1688 he was given a 22 gun salute from the ships in Port Royal harbour, and a lavish funeral.

The scale of these privateering operations in Caribbean waters did not leave the Cayman Islands untouched. Not only did the vessels and men taking part in the campaigns rendezvous at Cayman, some of them are reputed to have retired with their booty to these islands. As an authority on the sack of Panama has written:

> Most of the privateers did not follow their Admirall home to Jamaica .. Some sailed to leeward, some to windward, some went to search for more plunder, some for food, for supplies were now very short ... Many of the privateers never did come back to Jamaica, for a large number of Morgan's ships were wrecked on the Central American coast where they had gone to raid and look for food ... All but one of the remainder had appeared in Jamaica by early July ... Some of the Englishmen followed the Frenchmen back to Tortuga and Hispaniola, where an approximation to the old privateering life was to continue for many years into the future. One or two privateers set up as independent pirates off the south coast of Cuba or in the Cayman Islands, surreptitiously selling their prizes to their brethren in Jamaica. [11]

A number of the privateers who took part in Henry Morgan's expeditions – including such celebrated individuals as William Dampier and Exquemelin – clearly were familiar with the Cayman Islands, and their activities are detailed below. However, of more immediate import to the few settlers already resident on Cayman, was the Spanish reprisal for the excesses committed under the guise of English commissions by Morgan and his men.

A CORSAIR'S ATTACK ON CAYMAN: THE RIVERO PARDAL AFFAIR, 1670

The Spanish were not slow to seek revenge for Morgan's audacious and brutal attack on Portobello. Manoel Rivero Pardal, a Portuguese-born mercenary, received a privateering commission from the Governor of Cartagena on 3 January 1670. Three days later he set sail with a crew of 70 aboard his ship, the 'San Pedro y Fama'. Hoping to reach Port Morant, he was unable to sight his target, and instead, attacked the Cayman islands. Here he reportedly burnt a number of fishermen's shacks, took a ketch and a canoe, and kidnapped four children. [12]

RIVERO'S COMMISSION

Commission from Don Pedro de Ulloa Riva Deneyra, Governor and Captain General of Santiago, Carthagena and the Indies to Captain Manuel Rivero Pardal, with his frigate San Pedro y La fama to be Admiral against the English. Cartagena, 6 June 1670.

Several eye witnesses recorded their version of the events which subsequently occurred. Joan Boys was himself a prisoner of the Spanish, when, finding that he was a good pilot in the South Keys, he was sent on board Rivero's 8 gun frigate. He deponed that the Spanish captain's intention had been go to Port Morant "where he intended to steal 50 or 60 negroes and carry them to Havanna". Boys was promised a share for his part in the operation, but he recounted how, arriving instead off Cayman, *"he was sent on shoar to take an English prisoner, but being on shore advised the English of the Spanish intentions, and made his escape with the English, and only 4 children were taken prisoners by the Spanyards ..."*

If Boys is to be believed, his warning to the settlers on Cayman may have saved several lives. Julian Do Cobino made a similar statement to the effect that sent ashore to take prisoners, he had warned the English against the Spaniards and effected his own escape. However, the account of Cornelius Johnson, a Dutchman, who was on board the 'St Nicholas', one of the ships which sailed to Cayman, suggests that further casualties occurred. He reported *"that he heard the Spaniards brag that they put the English in the hold of the frigatte, nayled down the hatches, sett her on fire and burnt the English men alive in it, having given them quarter 14 days before"*. [13]

Samuel Hutchinson, commander of a ship at anchor in Hudson's Hole, Little Cayman on 14th April, with the 'Governor' of Cayman aboard his vessel, has provided the most detailed account of the attack. He reported seeing five ships

> *they appeared about four of ye clocke in the afternoone from the south part of ye Island, and came to an anchor within musket shott without ye Reefs of ye said Hudsons Hole with English colors flying, they firing six or seven guns shott at ye said Hutchinson's ship, upon which ye said Hutchinson hoisted his colors and fired one gun to leeward whereupon ye Spaniards loared ye English and hoisted the Burgonia flagg continued firing and manned ye tartan and severall boates in order to ye boarding ye said Hutchinson's ship, ... ye said Hutchinson lost only one man, though he had severall gun shott placed in the hull of his ship, his maine yard be-ing shot downe ... the Governor of ye Caymanns being then aboard, evening drawing on, went aboard their owne shipps and about 2 o clock of ye morning, ye Spaniards made false fires towards the north part of the Island, and in the meanewhile landed about two hundred men upon the easternmost part of the Island.*

Hutchinson added that he and the Governor eventually went on shore to prevent themselves being taken prisoner by the Spaniards and headed into the woods. Coming across some Spanish boats near the shore, *"demanding of them their Admiral's name and their reasons why they should come to destroy merchant men and fishermen"*, the Spaniards declined to reply. Having boarded Hutchinson's ship, the Spanish spent two days getting her off the rocks, and rigging her, leaving on the 17th with a ketch, the sloops and 18 prisoners.

French documents of the attack on Cayman specify that the Governor was ordinarily installed on the Brac. They also indicated that a ship of their nation had been in the vicinity at the time:

> *an old melancholic fool of an Englishman willingly left the King's service to settle on Cayman Brac, assuming the title of governor of the island, and ships that pass there salute him by that title as a kind of mockery. … 5 Spanish ships, along with some smaller boats, sailed by the Caymans; they may have planned to launch some assaults on the English, or may have taken this course by sheer chance as they headed for New Spain or Havana. This force sank the small boats of the English and captured and killed their crews, made up partly of pirates and partly of Jamaica residents. The Spaniards also showed their hostility by even burning the hut of the wretched Governor mentioned earlier. A ship from the city of Dieppe was then in the vicinity and it raised its colours to show that it was French. On seeing this, the commander of the five Spanish ships called back the boats that he had launched to deal with the French ship as they had dealt with the English. The Spaniards then left without further incident.* [14]

The placing of the settlement and the corsair attack at Little Cayman rather than the Brac has recently been bolstered by archaeological remains recovered from South Hole Sound, Little Cayman (see Chapter Five).

Rivero next made for Cuba, where he was informed that an English privateer ship, the 'Mary and Jane', was lying in the roads at Manzanillo. The commander, a Dutchman called Bernard Claesen Speirdyke, known as Captain Bart, put up a heroic resistance against Rivero's attack, killing up to one third of Rivero's men and losing four of his crew, before finally surrendering his own life. Nine prisoners were conveyed back to Port Royal with word of Rivero's commission. The ship's purser, Cornelius Carssen, specified that the 'Mary and Jane' had ironically been carrying letters to the Spanish announcing peace when the attack occurred.

Governor Sir Thomas Modyford reported on the incident in March 1670, noting *"this has so incensed the whole body of privateers, that he hears they meditate revenge, and have appointed a general rendezvous at Caimanos next month where he shall send to divert them or moderate their councils"*. Lord Arlington confined his response to the not irrelevant observation that Rivero's attack was *"not at all to be wondered at after such hostilities as your men have acted upon their territories"*. [15]

Rivero had meanwhile returned in triumph on 23 March to Cartagena, where a fiesta was organised, and he was rewarded with the royal standard for his ship. He embarked on a second cruise at the end of May, with 'La Gallardina,' a captured French ship. Appearing off the coast of Jamaica on 11 June 1670, Rivero captured the sloop of William Harris, reportedly hurling insults such as 'dogs and rogues' at the Englishmen. A week later he attacked Montego Bay, landing 30 men and burning the settlement. Early in July, Rivero was once again seen off Jamaica, landing long enough to commit further arson attacks and to post an infamous challenge.

RIVERO'S CHALLENGE

I, CAPTAIN MANUEL RIVERO PARDAL, TO THE CHIEF OF THE SQUADRON OF PRIVATEERS IN JAMAICA. I AM HE WHO THIS YEAR HAVE DONE THAT WHICH FOLLOWS. I WENT ON SHORE AT CAIMANOS AND BURNT 20 HOUSES, AND FOUGHT WITH CAPTAIN ARY, AND TOOK FROM HIM A CATCH LADEN WITH PROVISIONS AND A CANOA. AND I AM HE WHO TOOK CAPT BAINES, AND DID CARRY THE PRIZE TO CARTAGENA, AND NOW AM ARRIVED TO THIS COAST, AND HAVE BURNT IT. AND I COME TO SEEK GENERAL MORGAN, WITH TWO SHIPS OF 20 GUNS, AND HAVING SEEN THIS, I CRAVE HE WOULD COME OUT UPON THE COAST AND SEEK ME, THAT HE MIGHT SEE THE VALOUR OF THE SPANIARDS. AND BECAUSE I HAD NO TIME I DID NOT COME TO THE MOUTH OF PORT ROYAL TO SPEAK BY WORD OF MOUTH IN THE NAME OF MY KING, WHOM GOD PRESERVE. DATED THE 5TH OF JULY 1670.

Morgan and his consorts took the bait and sallied forth once again. One of the privateer commanders, Captain John Morris, in charge of a small 9 or 10 gun frigate, the 'Dolphin', was anchored off Cuba when Rivero arrived, on yet another mission. In the ensuing battle, Rivero *"was shot through the neck and immediately died, all his men jumped over board and were killed a great many of them in the water, only 4 or 5 of them hid themselves in the hold and were saved"*. The Governor could not conceal his satisfaction in the despatch which reported this capture:

> *Capt Morrice, driven by wind into a bay at the East end of Cuba, found Signor Pardal, the vapouring Admiral of St Jago .. At the first volley the Spaniards left their guns, and the captain running to bring them back, was killed by a shot in the throat, after which the men leapt overboard and about 40 came short home, and the vessel with 5 prisoners was carried to the Admiral.*

The commission, noted the Governor, revealed the status of Rivero for the Spanish, while his challenge, nailed to a tree on Jamaica, was indicative of his vanity. Also found among Rivero's papers was the following poem:

RIVERO'S POEM

[SETTING] SAILS AND PLOUGHING
THE DEEP SEA TO CAYMAN,
I MADE A DESTRUCTION OF FIRE,
BURNED HOUSES AND CAUSED RUIN,
WITH MY VALOROUS BREAST,
UNTIL ALL THE MULTITUDE,
[WAS TERRIFIED] BY MY NAME ALONE ... [16]

Meanwhile Morris brought Rivero's frigate to Morgan who added her to his fleet, and the incident which led to the first recorded full scale battle on Cayman became just a footnote in the increasingly ambitious activities of the English privateers.

WRECKS, RUNAWAYS AND RECRUITS: PRIVATEERS IN CAYMAN, 1671-1672

While Henry Morgan's men, having sacked Portobello, organised themselves for another enterprise against the Spaniards in the autumn of 1668, Richard Browne, a ship's surgeon, was sailing towards Jamaica from England in HMS Oxford. The 34-gun frigate had been sent from England on patrol duty for the colony, arriving in Jamaica on 14th October. Whilst the 'Oxford' was being prepared to undertake a six month cruise, carrying a crew of 160, a replacement commander was urgently appointed, in the words of Browne: *"in the place of Capt Hackit, who came out of England with her, but falling out with the master run him through the body, whereof he died, and then fled for it"*. Following this unfortunate and fatal duel, Captain Edward Collier took over the command of the 'Oxford', setting out in her on 20 December 1668. [17]

The Oxford's troubles were not over, however. Having anchored at the Ile a Vache off Hispaniola, towards the close of 1669, the frigate fell in company with the several English and French privateers already assembled there. As Browne recounted:

> *A Council of War was held aboard the Oxford on 2d January by Admiral Morgan and 8 others when they designed to attack Cartagena with the ships they had ... While the captains were at dinner on the quarter-deck the Oxford blew up, when 200 men were lost, including Captain Aylett, Commander of the Lilly, and Captains Bigford, Morris, Thornbury, and Whiting, only 6 men and 4 boys being saved. The accident is supposed to have been caused by the negligence of the gunner. I was eating my dinner with the rest, when the mainmasts blew out, and fell upon Captains Aylett, Bigford and others, and knocked them on the head; I saved myself by getting astride the mizen-mast.* [18]

The loss of such an important force prevented the privateers from putting their plan of taking Cartagena into execution. Richard Browne, meanwhile, was himself becoming increasingly frustrated. He reported that in 18 months' cruising (since February 1669) he had seen few Spanish ships, due, as he complained, to a "dull and sluggish commander, who made it not his business to cruse but lye in holds", and to the fact that the Spaniards were principally sailing in fleets. Having spent what Browne considered to be an excessive time in the Bay of Campeche, and Havana, the ship running out of provisions *"we went towards the Camanas to make some turtle where we found orders from Thomas Modyford Governor of Jamaica, to make all speed in for Jamaica, when we found that Sir Thomas had made peace with the Spaniards"* in May 1669. However in reprisal for the Spanish attack on Cayman, Browne reported , "the Governor and Council have made war with them, and Admiral Morgan is preparing a fleet with 1,500 men for some notable design on land". Browne now joined Morgan's men as Surgeon General, promising to send to his correspondents "a true narrative" of his adventures with the privateers. [19]

In August 1670, therefore, Browne was among the 600 men who sailed from Port Royal in a fleet of 11 vessels. Scattered by a storm off Hispaniola, the fleet regrouped, and being joined by more privateers, had increased to 38 vessels and more than 2,000 men by December. It was the largest buccaneer enterprise ever mounted, and must have terrified the few Spaniards defending the tiny Providencia Island, when the fleet loomed up on 24th December. The small force defending the island quickly surrendered.

A few days later, a trio of ships, carrying 470 men, was detached from the fleet to mount an advance attack on San Lorenzo fort, which guarded the mouth of the Chagres River. The 10 gun 'Lilly', commanded by Richard Norman, the flagship 'Mayflower', led by Joseph Bradley and the 'Seviliaen', commanded by Dutchman Jelles de Lecat (often written as Yellows, or Yhallahs) were chosen for the task. Early January 1671 saw them before their target, but, unexpectedly reinforced, the garrison put up a heavy resistance. Bradley was shot in both legs in the resulting battles, and died just as Morgan's fleet was arriving. Norman took over command of the advance guard and installed a new buccaneer force in the garrison.

The 'Lilly', returning from Chagres, stopped at the Cayman Islands, where disaster struck. The frigate was wrecked. Norman managed to carry off his guns, rigging and tackle, leaving the 'Lilly', behind. She was soon put to good use however, as another of Morgan's privateer captains, Morris, also turned up in Cayman, and his own ship being even more damaged than the 'Lilly', used what he saved from her to refit the latter. Morris then took on board between 30 and 40 privateers whom he found on Cayman and set off for the South Keys of Cuba.

The new privateer crew, recruited on Cayman, now turned pirate. As Governor Lynch of Jamaica later reported, having arrived at Cuba, Morris' men

> took a peragua laden with tobacco kept y men prysoners , tormented y men and divided y tobacco amongst them, y ship after this goes windward to y coast of Domingo there his men would have taken an English dogger boat, which they thought had 15,000 pieces of 8 in her, but he by force and a trick preventing it, they mutinied, carried him to ye Isla de Vaca, left him, and embarked on an English or French Pyrat, soe downe he came hither. But before he would come in, frankly confessed that his men had constrained him to take this peragua, and would have had him taken English too, because he would not left him, soe begged my pardon, which I assured him of, and to make my word good have paid to the Spaniards myselfe, and sent 100 pieces of 8 to him that is lamed. Yet thought it just to have both captain and ship tried in the Admiralty, where both were condemned for piracy. [20]

Pirogue Espagnole

A PERAGUA

(Labat, *Nouveau Voyage*, 1727)

Nevertheless, given the exigencies of the time, the Governor quickly pardoned Captain Morris, and as part owner of the Lilly, allowed him to sail again in her, once she had been "fitted and manned in the King's service". Despite his previous act of piracy the Governor expressed his confidence in Morris as *"a very stout fellow and good pilot, [who] will not turn pirate"*. Having thus escaped execution for his own act of piracy, Captain John Morris was now again on official duty as a privateer, and on a salary of 80 livres a month. This old hand with Henry Morgan, and the man who had trounced Rivero Pardal, was sent to the South Keys of Cuba and to the island of Triste to capture his errant former comrades, in a classic poacher turned gamekeeper scenario.

Chief among those whom Morris was instructed to seek out was the former privateer, Jelles, who had failed to return from the privateering mission undertaken with Morgan's men.
Suspecting that Jelles was holed up in the Cayman Islands, the Governor ordered Captain John Erasmus, his former partner, to go to Cayman in pursuit of the Dutchman, and to bring him and his ship back to Jamaica. Captain Henry Wills, on his return to Jamaica from Panama was asked by Erasmus for his brigantine "for the use of the Governor".

Morgan Jones was at anchor at Little Cayman, when Captains Erasmus and Jelles came aboard his vessel *"showed him an order from Sir Thomas Modyford, brought by Captain Erasmus, requiring Yhallah to repair to his commission port, and desired him to write an answer, which he did"*. [21]

By October 1671 Jelles was the only privateer who had failed to come in, following the action against Panama City and HMS Assistance had been sent after him "with orders to make examples of those rogues". The 'Assistance' followed Jelles to the Bay of Campeche, but found the Dutchman's vessel "so far in with the shore that the frigate could not command him". By December Jelles, along with two other privateers, Captains Diego and Martin, was still at large, and HMS Welcome had joined the search.

On 24th December 1671 the Governor was informed that Jelles had *"sold his frigate for 7,000 pieces of 8 to the Governor of Campeachy, and having put the English ashore, with the Dutch and French has entered into Spanish pay, and is fitting with two Spanish to take the logwood cutters. Jamaica has there four or five ships and as many barques"*. [22]

As Richard Browne reported to his correspondent, Joshua Williamson, on 30 January 1672, this was exactly what Jelles had intended. Using his English colours, he had *"taken 5 ships laden with logwood, one burnt, another sunk, and one belonging to Mr Bent, of London"*. It was believed that Jelles intended to take them to the Spanish, to make his peace with them. He was also accused of having gone ashore on the island of Triste, where he *"disarmed 30 or 40 English, that would have had him come to this port"*.

John Bant, master of the Hopewell, was present when the logwood ships were taken by Jelles, now acting for the Spanish. He reported that he was in the harbour of Boakonune on 11 December 1671 with three other vessels,

> when Capt Yellows' war canoe came up the harbour and boarded the ships, but having heard that Yellows had revolted to the Spaniard, Bant told them to keep off or he would fire. On the 12th Capt Yellows came up with them, having the English ensign flying, and told informant he was his prisoner, and that he had a commission from the Spaniard to take all Englishmen on that coast; so he surprised those four vessels and a New Englandman. On the 16th Yellows sailed with his five prizes for Campeachy, but turned informant and another ashore on the island that makes the harbour, where informant found a piece of a canoe, in which he went to the head of the river, where he found three small vessels of Jamaica, in one of which he got passage. [23]

While Jelles still held out, one of his consorts was captured. On 20 March 1672, aboard HMS Assistance, the Governor of Jamaica, together with Major Beeston, Commander of HMS Assistance and two other captains, deliberated at the trial of Captain Francis Witherborn for piracy. He was accused as follows:

> *That having notice of the Peace, he took command of the bark Charity to continue privateering, that he consorted with Yhallahs and fled when chased by the Assistance; that he took a Spanish canoa, and his mate Thomas Wright took another canoa which is still out privateering; that there were articles of consortship between Witherborn and one Captain De Mangle, a Frenchman, obliging each other to continue privateering; and that he would not have surrendered if not forced. To which Witherborn only made this defence, that his men governed him, that his mate Wright had greater influence over them than he had, and that the articles were only to blind the Frenchman. Upon consideration of the whole matter all were of opinion that having committed piracy and broken the articles of peace, Captain Witherborn ought to suffer death according to the law.* [24]

Jelles, now under commission to the Spanish Governor of Campeche, was acquiring "no small reputation among the Spaniards". He was believed to be the 'chief contriver' in the taking of a Dutch ship of 32 guns captured by surprise attack while trading near Campeche. By August 1672, the Spanish Ambassador was being asked to obtain satisfaction for the British prisoners taken by Jelles and still being held in confinement. [25]

In September 1672, however, Richard Browne informed Williamson that Captain Morris had also proved false. Pretending to set out for the island of Triste in pursuit of Jelles, Morris "*never attempted to pursue him though at Villa de Mores 70 leagues from him, but has laden his frigate with logwood*". Despite taking a salary from the Governor of Jamaica, Captain Morris had not only failed to bring in the Dutch privateer, but had used his cruise to enrich himself and his crew by amassing a cargo of logwood! Meanwhile, Jelles continued his depredations. By October, the Governor of Jamaica was ruefully admitting that Jelles had surprised 12 or 14 vessels cutting logwood, and that he had been obliged to take "*no notice, because he only connives at the wood cutting, and without orders dare not direct the retaking of our ships"*. Jelles, as a privateer now working for the Spanish, was acting with impunity, and the logwood trade, so important to Jamaica was under severe risk. [26]

A BARQUE

- the type of vessel engaged in the logwood trade.

(Labat, 1727).

Captains in the logwood trade like the Coxen brothers, Philip Osborne, John Mitchell and James Risby testified that they had been involved in the trade some 3 years with the 100 or so English residents on the coast of Yucatan, and had met with no obstruction until Jelles had begun to harass them. In early November 1672 the Governor issued instructions that the cutters should henceforth go out in fleets of at least four vessels, and was writing that the logwood trade was *"likely to be interrupted by a pirate that is fled to the Spaniards, and has already taken 14 vessels, and by capers from Curacoa, as well as three small frigates from Biscay, who are sent to clear that coast".* [27]

By mid 1673 Jelles was being assisted in his work by a renegade
Irishman Fitzgerald who had reportedly seized more of the Jamaica
vessels and even hanged an Englishman *"because he ran away from
the pirate Yhallahs and would not rob his countrymen"*. In
February 1674, Fitzgerald and Jelles were still at large, and it was
decided to issue a Proclamation forbidding them to serve any
foreign Prince, recommending that the men be offered a pardon if
they came in, while if they failed to give themselves up, the
Governor of Jamaica should *"receive speedy order for securing both
said persons if found so offending after the time limited within his
Government, and cause them to be sent prisoners to England".* [28]

PRIVATEERS AND EXPLORERS' ACCOUNTS
OF CAYMAN FLORA AND FAUNA

If privateers like Captain James Morris, and Jelles de Lecat were
frequently tempted into piracy and became outlaws and torturers,
others were gentlemen and men of letters, who, while engaged in the
maritime adventuring of their day, exhibited a curiosity for, interest
in, and penchant for recording the wonders they saw in their
voyages. If indeed, the tales of a buccaneer like Exquemelin may
have been 'enhanced' from the memoirs of others, the credentials of
individuals like William Dampier cannot be doubted.

William Dampier

The son of a tenant farmer from Somerset, Dampier was
apprenticed in 1669 to a master mariner, and sailed to France
and Newfoundland. In 1671 he voyaged aboard an East Indiaman
to Bantam as a foremast hand. After a period of service aboard HMS
Royal Prince, Dampier went to Jamaica, sailing with buccaneers
between 1679 and 1688, during which he participated in the raid on
Porto Bello. [29]

WILLIAM DAMPIER

Dampier first mentions visiting the Cayman Islands in 1675. In August of that year, he left Port Royal in a small Jamaica bark, in the company of a New England ketch, for the Bay of Campeche on a logwood trading voyage. The bark made the passage in under 2 weeks, landing at Triste Island in the bay. On the way, Dampier reported, *"we sailed by little Caimanes, leaving it on our Larboard-side and Key Monbrack, which are two small Islands, lying South of Cuba"*.

The vessels were carrying rum and sugar to trade with the 250 logwood cutters working there, and Dampier mentions that on imbibing the punch the cutters "grew Frolicksome". Evidently the crew sampled their own cargo, for he notes "on Board the Vessels we were loud enough till all our Liquor was spent". Visiting the loggers' huts, Dampier mentions that *"we were always very kindly entertain'd with pig and pork, and pease, or beef and dough-boys .. As long as the Liquor lasted, which they bought of us, we were treated with it, either in Drams or Punch"*.

In September 1675 Dampier's bark returned to Triste island to water, setting sail two days later. On this occasion, weather conditions were less favourable, and Dampier reports that the passage took 13 weeks, as *"the vessel would not ply to windward and was driven upon several shoals"*. During the voyage they were spotted by the Spanish who chased them all night in a three-masted ship, but they managed to elude capture.

Shortly afterwards, they narrowly avoided grounding their vessel on the Alacran reefs. Skirting Cuba, they had now been about two months on the passage since leaving Triste when they

> *fell in with the West-end of Grand Caymanes. This island is about 40 leagues South from Pines, and about 15 to the West of little Caymanes. We anchored at the West-end, about half a Mile from the Shore. We found no Water nor any Provision, but saw many Crocodiles on the Bay, some of which would scarce stir out of the way for us. We kill'd none of them (which we might easily have done) though Food began to be short with us; indeed had it been in the Months of June or July we might probably have gotten Turtle, for they frequent this Island some Years as much as they do little Caymanes. We stayed here but 3 or 4 Hours, and steered back for Pines, intending there to hunt for Beef or Hog, of both of which there is in great plenty.* [30]

Fear of the Spaniards cut short their stay on the Isle of Pines, where they captured and killed a hog, but jettisoned some of the meat in order to proceed more quickly to the safety of the shore. Although they had a good roast dinner that night, their provisioning proved scarce sufficient for the remainder of the voyage. Dampier records eking out a scant diet with boiled beef which *"though it did not stink, yet it was very unsavoury and black"*. Fortunately, at this low ebb in their fortunes, the welcome landmark of Bluefields Hill on Jamaica was sighted and the next day Dampier and his fellow travellers anchored at Negril, having been 13 weeks on the passage. Dampier wryly comments: *"I think never any Vessel before nor since, made such Traverses in coming out of the Bay as we did, having first blunder'd over the Alcrany Riff, and then visited those*

Islands; from thence fell in among the Colorado Shoals, afterward made a Trip to Grand Caymanes; and lastly, visited Pines, tho' to no Purpose. In all these Rambles we got as much Experience as if we had been sent out on a Design".

Among Dampier's observations on the flora and fauna of the Caribbean islands, are several passages which reflect his stay on Grand Cayman. He noted, *"At the Isle Grand Caymmanes, there are Crocodiles, but no Alligators".* Dampier distinguished crocodile flesh as having a less musky flavour than alligator meat, whilst the latter had four distinctive 'kernel' or growths which exuded a strong musky odour. He noted however that the Spanish called both species 'Caymanes'. [31]

Given that, at the time of Dampier's voyages, turtle flesh was an important supplement to a sailor's diet while cruising in the Caribbean, it is not surprising that he discusses this meat, and its supposed restorative properties, at length. He noted that a taste for the meat was not shared by all nationalities. The Spanish and Portuguese, were not fond of turtles, for example:

Nay they have a great Antipaty against them, and would much rather eat a Porpoise, tho' our English count the green Turtle very extraordinary Food ... many of our English Valetudinarians have gone from Jamaica (tho' there they have also turtle) to the I. Caimanes, at the Laying-time, to live wholly upon Turtle that then abound there; purposely to have their Bodies scour'd by this Food, and their Distempers driven out; and have been said to have found many of them good Success in it. [32]

Dampier was particularly struck by the turtle's breeding habits :

There are 4 sorts of Sea-turtle,, viz. the Trunk-turtle, the Loggerhead, the Hawks-bill and the Green-turtle ... One thing is very strange and remarkable in these Creatures; that at the breeding time they leave for 2 or 3 Months their common haunts, where they feed most of the Year, and resort to other places, only to lay their Eggs: And 'tis not thought that they eat any thing during this Season; So that both He's and She's grow very lean; but the He's to that degree that none will eat them. The most remarkable places that I did ever hear of for their breeding, is at an Island in the West Indies called Caimanes, and the Isle Ascension in the Western Ocean: and when the breeding time is past, there is none remaining. Doubtless they swim some hundreds of Leagues to come to those two places: For it hath been often observed, that at Caimanes, at the breeding time there are found all those sorts of Turtle before described. The South Keys of Cuba are above 40 leagues from thence, which is the nearest place that these Creatures can come from; and it is most certain, that there could not live so many there as come here in one Season". [33]

EXQUEMELIN AND THE HABITS OF THE CAYMAN TURTLE

*These creatures have certain customarry places whither they repair every year to lay their eggs. The chiefest of these places are the three islands called Caymanes ..
It is a thing muchh deserving consideration how the tortoises can find out these islands. For the greatest part of them come from the Gulf of Honduras, distant thence the whole space of 150 leagues. Certain it is, that many times the ships, having lost their latitude through the darkness of the weather, have steered their course only by the noise of tortoises swimming that way, and have arrived unto those isles. When their season of hatching is past, they retire towards the island of Cuba, where are many good places that afford them food. But while they are at the islands of Caymanes, they eat very little or nothing.*

(Exquemelin, *Boucaniers of America*, p 61-2)

FRENCH AND ENGLISH PRIVATEER CONFLICTS AT CAYMAN, 1680-1682

Despite the English presence on nearby Jamaica, and the one-time siting of a nominal Governor to represent their interests on Cayman, attacks by Spanish shipping, and the increasing resort to the islands by renegade privateers and pirates, led to a calling-in of the English settlers there. As a result, the French, long-time consumers of the abundant turtle of Cayman, were able to re-establish a presence in the region.

By 1680, when the San Antonio de Padua captured a French ship off Grand Cayman, the Spanish considered that 'Cayman Chico' had become the headquarters of French corsairs who cruised the waters between Grand and Little Cayman The French retorted that their ships were merely in the region for the purpose of catching turtle, however, other sources confirm the likelihood that French privateers were using Cayman as a base at this time. [34]

In May 1681, another French turtler came to grief, this time at the hands of an English privateer, off Cayman. Captain Herbouin of 'La Royale', travelling from St. Christopher, carrying salt and brandy, stopped to collect turtles at Cayman, when, 2 leagues from those islands, he was met by an English ship, armed with several cannon and with a crew of 50 men, who fired on him, and declared that in view of the war between their nations, his ship was being taken as a prize. Offloaded onto the long boat with 5 men, a barrel of water, and a few pounds of salted turtle, Herbouin and the little group survived for 3 weeks on an islet, subsisting on fruits and roots, before finding their way to Jamaica and from there to France. [35]

In the following year, Pierre Ubinet confessed to being a French pirate, with a commission from Tortuga, after he was captured by the Spanish near Carthagena. He informed them that Cayman was used by French pirates as a base, and that they would work together with English pirates, raiding Spanish settlements, sometimes guided by local Indians. [36]

CAPTAIN JOSEPH BANNISTER:
A PIRATE CAPTURED IN CAYMAN, 1684

Captain Bannister was the commander of a merchantman, the 'Golden Fleece'. In June 1684 he fled Port Royal in his 30 gun ship, recruited more than a hundred men, from sloops and from other islands and, allegedly armed with a French commission, set off on a privateering venture.

Bannister's renegade voyage in the Golden Fleece soon ended in disaster. The HMS Ruby and the HMS Boneta, cruising off Jamaica on the look-out for pirates, captured Bannister while he was stocking up with turtle at the Cayman Islands on 27 July. As the Governor of Jamaica reported the event:

> *last night the Ruby brought in Bannister. He took him at Caymanos; he has about 115 men on board, most the veriest roghues in these Indies. I have ordered the ship and men to be delivered into the Admiralty and commanded the judge immediately to proceed against them, because we do not know how to secure or keep such a number. We conclude they'll be found guilty of pyracy.* [37]

However, as Colonel Molewsorth later reported, it was found that Bannister was in fact without a commission - the Governor of Hispaniola having refused him one. He had nevertheless captured two Spaniards, found prisoners aboard the 'Golden Fleece'. But the Spaniards declined to take the matter further so that 'the grand jury threw out the bill' of piracy. The condition of the ailing Governor, Lynch, was reportedly aggravated by this reversal, which 'much increased his disease' and he died on 24 August. Sir Hender Molesworth who took over, sought to gain a conviction, but the Spaniards did not prove helpful, they 'swear backward and forward', as the new Governor complained, and utimately in September 1684 Bannister was bound over and ordered to appear at the next court. [38]

Bannister was naturally unwilling to await the further attempts of the Jamaican administration to convict him, and began making secret preparations to flee the island a second time. Thus in late January 1685 he escaped from the Port Royal gaol, seized a sloop and passed 14 guns pointing out towards the bay before the commander of the fort, Major Peter Beckford, became aware of the attempted escape, and ordered Bannister's sloop to be fired upon. Despite suffering at least three direct hits, the sloop was not crippled. Bannister had been prepared, having ordered 50 men into the hold, equipped with plugs to stop any holes which appeared.

The daring escape was recounted by the weary Molesworth:

> *on a dark night in a desperate resolute manner Bannister past the fort, having provided himself of plugs of all sizes wherewith to stop any breach which could be made in him by the guns of the fort, for which he had (as is sayd) about 50 men in the hold that stood ready. But what by the carelessness of the sentrys and the darkness of the night, being favoured also with a freshe land brieze, he was got abrest of the fort before Major Beckford that commands it had any notice given to him ... Beckford did all that he could, but only placed three shot in him. He at once sent me word of the occurrence, which was a great surprize to me, for I thought that Bannister's want of credit would prevent him from ever getting the ship to sea again ... yet now he has obtained credit from some persons underhand, and has his ship well fitted out in every respect. It was done so artfully that no one suspected it, or I should have found some pretext for securing him.* [39]

Molesworth sent HMS Boneta after the Golden Fleece, but Captain Stanley "findng hmself unable to do more against a ship of her size and strength", merely gave Bannister a note warning him that he would be treated as a pirate if he did not return. Bannister's reply was that he had "done no pyratical act as yet and intended to do none, but his design was for the bay of Honduras for logwood." Bannister was next seen in April 1685, in company with the privateers Laurens, Yankey, Jacobs and Grammont, off the Ile a Vache. The Commander of HMS Ruby demanded Bannister from Grammont, as serving under a foreign commission, but was informed that Bannister had not entered the French king's service.

In November 1685 Bannister was spotted again, cruising leeward of Jamaica and, following this latest sighting, Commander Mitchell of HMS Ruby, then being careened, volunteered to take two hired sloops, manned by his crew, to go after Bannister. No further sightings were made for six months, but it was evident that he was still out capturing ships. In May 1686 one of his victims reported to Molesworth that the 'Golden Fleece' was careening off the eastern end of Hispaniola, near the Gulf of Samana. HMS Falcon and HMS Drake had by now replaced the Ruby on patrol duties, and their captains Charles Talbot and Thomas Spragg, finally intercepted Bannister. However his careening place was fortified, and a battle ensued:

> *on June 24th the Falcon and Drake frigates found the chief*
> *buccaneer Bannister with two ships in a deep bay fit to go on the*
> *careen at Jamana on the north side of Hispaniola, having got his*
> *guns on shore and mounted them in two batteries. The frigates*
> *stood in, though they were warmly entertained for two hours from*
> *the batteries and with small shot from the hips, and, bringing all*
> *their guns to bear, sunk and beat almost to pieces the buccaneer's*
> *ships, but not having enough water to carry them in, the Drake*
> *having but eleven foot, they could not fire them. The Drake had 13*
> *killed and wounded and the Falcon 10.* [40]

The captains were reprimanded at Port Royal for not destroying the pirate ship, despite the fact that they had been under heavy fire and had run out of ammunitions. They refitted, and set sail again early in July to finish the job of destroying Bannister. On returning to the Gulf of Samana they found that Bannister had burnt his ship and sailed away in a smaller vessel. Eventually Captain Spragg succeeded in capturing Bannister, as the log of HMS Falcon reported on 28 January 1687 *"this day the Drake arrived, with Banister; he and 3 of his partners hanged at the yards arms, and severall other prisoners"* .

The sight of the pirates' bodies dangling from HMS Drake was warmly applauded by the Governor who considered it a speedier and more definite course of justice than a further trial for Bannister. Molesworth thus described it as good lesson for the

> *favourers of pirates, the manner of his punishment being that which will most discourage others, which was the reason why I empowered Captain Spragge to inflict it. Bannister seemed to have no small confidence in his friends; I find from letters that he wrote to some of them that he intended to plead that he had been forced into all that he had done by the French. How far this would have prevailed with a Port Royal jury I know not, but I am glad that the case did not come before one.* [41]

GRAMMONT

GRAMMONT, VAN HOORN, DE GRAAF AND YANKY, 1682-1686

Joseph Bannister and William Dampier, in their voyages across the Caribbean, had at various times fallen in with a group of French and Dutch privateers whose exploits against the Spanish at Vera Cruz and Campeche, were as daring as the campaigns of Henry Morgan some years earlier. Once again, Cayman was used as a rendezvous and victualling point as the privateers massed, caroused, disputed and dispersed during the campaigns.

Accounts of the lives and exploits of these privateers, like those of the English buccaneers, are laced with more than a dash of glamour and heroism, with perhaps as much imagination as accuracy in their making. Grammont was said to be from southwest France, and to have been born a gentleman. Reportedly sent to sea at the age of 14, after killing his sister's suitor in a duel, he was later involved in the taking of a rich Dutch merchantman off Martinique which netted him a handsome sum. That which made him notorious, it is recorded, is that he spent the enormous sum of 80,000 livres in 8 days. However, gambling his last stash of booty, he won enough to buy a vessel armed with 50 cannons. He came to Tortuga to engage a crew, and subsequently conducted four expeditions which secured his reputation: Maracaibo in 1678, Cumana in 1680, Vera Cruz in 1682 and Campeche in 1686. His men gained little from the first of these expeditions to Maracaibo: L'Olonnois and Morgan having already squeezed the hapless denizens. [42]

DIVIDING THE SPOILS

(La Croix, *Histoire de la Piraterie*)

Meanwhile, Dutchman Laurens Cornelis Boudewijn de Graaf was also making a name for himself as a leader of the buccaneers of Samana Bay. Born in Holland, and for several years a gunner in Spain's Armada, de Graaf deserted in the Antilles, and began cruising on his own account from around 1676. He took the usual career route of pirates – capturing a small bark, and then a bigger vessel until he eventually secured a ship of more than 24 guns, the 'Tigre', from the Spanish in the autumn of 1679. Depicted as tall, with a handsome face, and blond hair, and a Spanish style moustache, De Graaf was said to be known among the flibustiers for his politeness and good taste. His ship always carried violins and trumpets with which he liked to entertain his guests.

Like De Graaf, Nikolaas van Hoorn was another Dutch adventurer with French ties. Reputedly swarthy of complexion and small in stature, Van Hoorn was a former sailor, who having amassed 200 ecus, went to France to seek a commission as a privateer. He purchased a small boat with a fellow mariner, and assembled a crew of 25 to 30 men. Disguising it as a fishing boat, he succeeded in taking several Dutch prizes before trading in his ship for a man of war. In autumn 1681, in command of the British slaving vessel the 'Mary and Martha' of 400 tons, and carrying 40 guns, Van Hoorn turned two of the merchants ashore at Cadiz, stealing Spanish guns, and looting slaves from the Dutch at Guinea. [43]

Following Van Hoorn's depredations, through news brought in by Jamaican fishing vessels, the Governor of Jamaica noted that, sent by the French after La Trompeuse and other pirates, Van Hoorn had instead gone to Cayman, where he reportedly *"spoke with some pryvateers and sent for others to meet him in y Bay of Honduras"*.

In fact, preparations were underway for an assault on Vera Cruz. At a gathering at Roatan, which included Grammont and De Graaf, the plan was discussed. Another Dutch privateer, Yanky, along with the Jamaican George Spurre and Jacob Hall of Virginia, were recruited. Eventually a pirate fleet of 5 ships and 8 smaller craft and a band of

more than a 1,000 men approached Vera Cruz on 17th May.
Marching stealthily under cover of darkness towards the city, the
raiders attacked at dawn. As the Governor of Jamaica later reported:

> *they came y latter end of May on y coast of La Vera Cruz, and there*
> *put 800 men into Yankyes, and another ship, these approached the*
> *coast, and by a mistake (as fatal as that at Honduras) y Spaniards on*
> *shoare took them for 2 of y flota, so made fires to pylot them,*
> *without sending to see, or know who they were, by which meanes*
> *they landed in y night and being but 2 miles from y towne, by breake*
> *of day came into it, tooke 2 forts of 12 and 16 guns, finding centinels*
> *and soldiers asleepe and y people in their houses as quiet and still as*
> *if in theyre graves, til they wakened them by breaking open theyr*
> *doores, ... they had a quiet plundering of churches, houses and*
> *convents for 3 days and not finding gold and silver enough, they*
> *threatened to burn y great church, and as the prysoners were over*
> *60000 so then they sent into y country for money and gave them, so*
> *the fourth day they left y town, and went with their pillage to a cay,*
> *and there divided it ... They brought away abundance of negroes,*
> *mulattoes and mesteios. In the action the Spaniards killed but one*
> *man ... Van Horn talks of going for Petit Guane but cannot get*
> *thyther without careening so sayd he would go for New England,*
> *Jacob Hall is gone to Carolina, Yancky got first to Caymanas and is*
> *bound for Spaniola.* [44]

Ironically, this was to be Van Hoorn's last escapade; he died a
fortnight after the sack of Vera Cruz, not from a wound inflicted by
the Spanish, but from a blow inflicted by his colleague, De Graaf.
Awaiting a ransom at Sacrificios Island, Van Hoorn had threatened to
decapitate some of his Spanish prisoners, which De Graaf opposing,
they had drawn swords, and the former had suffered a cut on the
wrist. The wound became infected, and Van Hoorn died off Isla
Mujeres. The flamboyant Van Hoorn who was said to wear a
necklace of large pearls with a beautiful ruby, reportedly died a
wealthy man, leaving his Ostend-based widow to enjoy the fruits of
his plunder. [45]

In September 1683 the Jamaican Governor was reporting that Van Hoorn's ship had gone to Hispaniola while rumours abounded as to the future of De Graaf:

> *Some fancy he has a mind to leave the French and his trade, and come and settle here, for killing Van Horne has put him ill with the French, and the Government on the coast is mighty confused, ... withdrawing Lawrence would be a mighty service to y Spaniards, for if he appeases with y French, they'l goe neer to attacque.* [46]

In the event, however, Laurens De Graaf was pardoned for the murder of Van Hoorn, became a naturalised Frenchman and was named Commandant of Police at St Domingue. Later appointed a Chevalier de St Louis, he reportedly lived to play an active part in the wars against the English and is said to have been the founder of the city of Mobile in Louisiana before his death in 1704. Grammont, for his part, was also given a commission as Lieutenant du Roi. In October 1686, however, he left Tortuga with three ships and was never heard of again. [47]

Yankey, more at home in the waters around Jamaica and Cayman, continued to be a thorn in the side of the English settlers. In February 1684 he was in action with his fellow privateers again:

> *about the beginning of this month Grammont went in Vanhorn's ship to leeward, with 6 more, to join Laurens on the coast of the Main. For he, Yankey, and Mitchell went to Carthagena, where the Governor sent out two great ships, the Lapaz and the St Francisco, and a sloop to chase them away. All three of these ships, however, were taken by the pirates. The Lapaz fought and lost 80 men, and the St Francisco ran ashore ... The Ruby met some of them [the pirates] off Carthagena .... Captain Tennant says that Yankey showed him a commission from the Governor of Petit Guavos, who, I suppose, has had orders from Martinique to issue commissions.*

By the end of the year, Yankey was in trouble with the Jamaican authorities for having seized one of their sloops, and Captain Mitchell, a naval officer on HMS Ruby, was instructed to sail to

Petit Guavos and demand the handing over of Yankey as a pirate, or, if he should meet Yankey on his journey, to seize and bring him to Jamaica for trial. Meanwhile a formal complaint was made to the French Governor of Petit Guavos:

> the sloop James, was seized by Captain Yankey, a privateer belonging to your port, under French colours, who, having plundered the ship and kept the men prisoners for 6 weeks, at length carried them to Petit Guavos, where without proof of any kind the Intendant and Council condemned sloop and goods as lawful prize. I am surprised at this act of hostility, considering the friendly relations between the two crowns ... I hear that you so far disowned the proceedings of the Council as to refuse to accept the share due to you as Governor, so that you cannot but be sensible of the justice of my complaint. I hope therefore that you will give me satisfaction, as I should give it to you in the like case. [48]

Predictably, Boisseau, the French Governor of Petit Guavos, denied that Captain Yankey was a pirate: *"I assure you that we know him to be incapable of such a thing"*.

In September 1685 Governor Molesworth was reporting that *"from Petit Guavos we hear that the King of France has lately given very strict orders for the recall of all privateers from attack on the Spaniards, wherein hitherto they have been encouraged....being accustomed to live by rapine and hating honest labour, they cannot forsake their old practices, and we may find ourselves concerned"*. Grammont's men were reported to be in distress for food, but were refused trade with the English, while De Graaf was apparently heading for Tortuga. Yankey, it was said, had "taken a Spanish vessel with 50,000 dollars off Havana". [49]

By September 1687, however, luck seemed no longer to be on Yankey's side. He appeared off the coast of Jamaica begging to be supplied with victuals. This was refused. The Governor offered him an amnesty if he would come in, whilst at the same time instructing one of his naval captains to demand Yankey's surrender and to bring him into port. That officer's ship being incapacitated, nothing was done, until Yankey himself sent in a letter, asking to come in.

YANKEY'S LETTER

We have arrived from Carolina and brought several people thence who have been driven from the Colony by the trouble with the Spaniards. In all sincerity we present ourselves, our ships and company to the service of the King of
England, and hope for your assurance that our ships and men shall not be troubled or molested, as we are ignorant of the laws and customs of this island. We can satisfy

The conditions offered by the Governor, requiring them to break up their ships, were not to their liking, and Yankey limped off with his damaged ships, having lost most of his men to desertion. Another letter was subsequently sent in to the Governor:

> We have suffered much from calms and storms, and have only arrived after much distress off Point Negril. We beg you to consider that if our ships are broken up we shall be left destitute of all livelihood in present and future, and to allow us the use of them. We have neither of us money to purchase an estate ashore. I shall work into Bluefields and thence to Port Royal, but we are deserted by most of our men, and have none but raw hands left, so are afraid to stand close inshore for land winds.

The Governor was not to be swayed by these pleas, and Yankey and his partner were next heard of in February 1688, chasing a Spanish ship in the Bay of Honduras, which they captured. This was to be among the privateer's last successes, however, as by August the rump of his pirate company was in custody in Boston, and Yankey and Jacob were both confirmed to be dead. [50]

The privateers, if they were lucky, like Morgan and De Graaf, could end their lives as respected citizens, feted and awarded high honours. Most, however, trod a fine line between fighting for their country, and scrapping for dubious prizes, risking denunciation as pirates. Ever dependent on the volatile relationships between warring European nations, in times of peace, when their services were no longer required, habituated to robberies and raids, unable to adjust to settled life, they retreated to isolated outposts, ever a prey to hunger and disease. Cayman, only sporadically settled in the 17th century, was an ideal hide-out and haunt for privateers of many nations, as the numerous actions related in this chapter, which occurred around those shores, testify.

REFERENCES

1. J.B. Du Tertre *Histoire generale des Antilles Habitee par les Francais*, Volume 1, p. 173-186. See also K.E. Lane, *Blood and Silver A History of Piracy in the Caribbean and Central America*, p. 100; C.H. Haring, *The Buccaneers in the West Indies in the XVII Century*, p. 82-3.
2. The Blue Dove - Portuguese Commission (Letter of Marque) to Charles de Bils, 10 Feb 1658, 10 Sept 1662 [Mass. Archives, vol 60, p 215] as reproduced in J.F. Jameson, *Privateering and Piracy in the Colonial Period: Illustrative Documents*.
3. *The Deposition of Daniel Sprague, July 1664 [Mass. Archives, vol 60, p. 229], reproduced in ibid.*
4. Deposition of John Hunter, 26 July 1664 [MAss Archives vol 60 p 225], and Deposition of William Browne, 25 July 1664 [Mass Archives, vol 60 p 223], in ibid.
5. Deposition of Charles Hadsall, 27 July 1664 [Mass. Archives, vol 60 p. 231-2]; Petition of John Douglass, Aug 1664 and the Plea of John Douglass 8 Aug 1664, in ibid.
6. PRO CO 1/24 'A narrative of Sir Thomas Modyford, Governor of His Majesties Island of Jamaica, setting forth the grounds and reasons and the orders he had thereon, for graunting Commissions against the Spanyards', 23 Aug 1669.
7. CSP 1661-8 no 1147 8 March 1666 Modyford to Lord Arlington; no 1216. 16 June 1666. For further details of the privateers' actions see D. Marley, *Pirates: Adventurers of the High Seas*, p 36-38.

8. PRO CO 1/19 despatch of 20 April 1665 and see p. 280 'A true and perfect Narrative by Colonell Theodore Cary, declaring ye proceedings in y late expedition from this Island of Jamaica against y Dutch, under the management of Lt Generall Edward Morgan until his death, and afterward by Colonell Theodory Cary', 17 Nov. 1665; CSP 1661-68 no 1042 23 Aug 1665 Col. Theodore Cary, St Eustatius to Duke of Albemarle.

9. S. Johnson, *Sunken Ships and Treasures,* p. 404; D.F. Marley, op. cit., p. 48-65; J. Pascall, *Pirates and Privateers*, p. 34.

10. CSP 1661-68, no 1838. 7 Sept 1668 Port Royal. Information of Admiral Henry Morgan and his officers ... of their late expedition on the Spanish coast with the reasons of their late attempt on Porto Principe and Porto Bello; no 1850 Oct 1 1668. Governor Modyford to Duke of Albemarle; CSP 1669-1674 no 789 30 March 1672 Major James Banister to Lord Arlington.

11. P. Earle, *The Sack of Panama,* p. 245.

12. ibid., p. 148-152.

13. PRO CO 1/27 The Depositions of Johan Boys, Julian Do Cobino and of Cornelius Johnson, June 1670.

14. PRO CO 1/25 Deposition of Samuel Hutchinson, 16 June 1669/70. For the French reference, see CINA MSD 145 Translation of 'Des Isles Caymans' from Bibliotheque Nationale Paris, Departement des Manuscrits, Fond Colbert, vol 31, Receuil de Relations et Memoires sur l'Espagne, les Indes... [c. 1670], p. 622-623.

15. PRO CO 1/25 p. 54 The deposition of Cornelius Carssen purser of y shipp Mary and Jane; CSP 1669-74 no 161 March 18 1670 Modyford to Arlington; Arlington to Modyford 12 June 1670.

16. Rivero's challenge is in CSP 1669-74 no 310 (ii) and the commission and poem in PRO CO 1/25 p. 128-9v, and p. 157-8; see also the deposition of Richard Browne in PRO CO 1/25.

17. CSP 1661-68 no 1867, 9 Nov 1668, Port Royal. Richard Browne to Williamson; no 1892, 17 Dec 1668, Port Morant, Richard Browne, to Williamson.

18. CSP 1675-76 no 1207 Richard Browne to Joseph Williamson, 20 Jan 1669 Port Royal.

19. PRO CO 1/25 Depositions of Richard Brown 7 and 10 Aug 1670; and CSP 1669-1674 No 227 Aug 7 1670 Richard Browne to Williamson.

20. PRO CO 1/28 Lynch, Jan 1671 and see CSP 1669-74 no 742 Jan 27 1672 Sir Thomas Lynch to Joseph Williamson.

21. CSP 1669-74 no 705 21 Dec 1671 Minutes of the Council of Jamaica, Depositions of Henry Morgan, Capt Henry Wills, and Morgan Jones.

22. Pawson, M. & Buisseret, D. *Port Royal*, p. 33; CSP 1669-74 no 640 14 Oct 1671 Sir Thomas Lynch to the Earl of Sandwich; no 697 of 17 Dec 1671; no 709 25 Dec 1671 Sir Thomas Lynch to Lord Arlington .

23. CSP 1669-74 no 883 July 2 1672.

24. CSP 1669-74 no 1216 Richard Browne to Jos. Williamson, 30 Jan 1672 Port Royal; CSP 1669-74 no 785 20 March 1672 Minutes of a Council of War held aboard HMS Assistance at Jamaica.

25. CSP 1669-74 no 888 July 8 1672 Hender Molesworth to Thomas Duck; no 908 12 Aug 1672 Lord Arlington to Spanish Ambassador's Memorial of 17 July.

26. CSP 1669-74 no 940 28 Sept 1672 Richard Browne to Sir Joseph Williamson no 945 9 Oct 1672 Sir Thomas Lynch to Henry Slingesby.

27. CSP 1669-74 no 954 Lynch to Slingesby 5 Nov 1672.

28. CSP 1669-74 no 1115 8 July 1673 Sir Thomas Lynch to Dr Worsley; no 1226 27 Feb 1674 Petition of Thomas Jarvis and others to the King in Council. Enclosure 3 Minutes of the Committee for Trade and Plantations, March 10 1674.

29. For his own account of his life, see *Dampier's Voyages*, ed Masefield, J. London, 1906.

30. ibid., Vol 2, p. 114, 133-4.

31. ibid., Vol 2, p 175. For a long time, the early reports of crocodiles on Cayman were believed to have been the figment of travellers' imaginations, or a mistaken sighting of large iguanas. However, skeletons of Crocodylus acutus an American species associated with mangrove lagoons and tidal marshes have recently been found on Little Cayman, while on Grand Cayman, bone remains of a fresh-water species, associated with Cuba (Crocodylus rhombifer) which grows up to 15 feet in length have been found. See Smith, R.S. *The Maritime Heritage of the Cayman Islands*, p. 88.

32. ibid., Vol 2, p. 399.

33. ibid., Vol 1, p. 129-33.

34. CINA MSD 120.

35. PRO CO 1/47 p 137-8 Memorial of the French Ambassador, Barrillon, at Newmarket, 29 Sept 1681; see also CSP 1681-85 no 236.

36. CINA MSD 172 Confession dated 20 Feb 1682 by Pedro Ubinet.

37. CSP 1681-84 no 1759 Sir Thomas Lynch to the Lord President of the Council 20 June 1684.

38. CSP 1681-5 no 1852 Molesworth to Earl of Sunderland, 30 Aug 1684 and no 1867 of 19 Sept 1684.

39. Pawson, M. & Buisseret, D. *Port Royal, Jamaica*, p. 41-55.

40. CSP 1681-5 no 2067 3 Feb 1685; CSP 1685-8, no 193 of 15 May 1685; no 463 of 16 Nov 1685; CSP Domestic Series, James II vol ii, art 961.

41. 1685-8 no 754 and no 755 of 5 July 1686 and no 839 of 31 Aug 1686; PRO Adm 51/345 Log of Falcon 28 Jan 1687; CSP 1685-8 no 1127 of 9 Feb 1687.

42. Blond, G. *Histoire de la Flibuste*, p. 212-3.

43. Oexmelin, *Histoire des Aventuriers Flibustiers*, p. 276, p. 290-8; Marley, D. *Pirates*, p 73-4.

44. PRO CO 1/52 Despatch of Governor Lynch, Jamaica, 26 July 1683. See also CSP 1681-85 no 1163 Sir Thomas Lynch to Secretary Sir Leoline Jenkins, 26 July 1683.

45. Haring, C.H. *The Buccaneers in the West Indies in the XVII Century*, p. 241-2; D. Marley, *Pirates*, p 76-77; Oexmelin op. cit., p. 290-8.

46. CSP 1681-85 Lynch to the Committee, Jamaica, 12 Sept 1683.

47. Kemp, P.K. & Lloyd, C. *The Brethren of the Coast*, p. 73; Marley, op. cit., p. 82-85.

48. CSP 1681-1685 no 1563 28 Feb 1684 Sir Thomas Lynch to the Lords of Trade and Plantations; no 1958 23 Nov 1684 Instructions from Colonel Hender Molesworth to Captain Mitchell, RN, HMS Ruby; no 1964 26 Nov 1684. Jamaica, Colonel Hender Molesworth to the Governor of Petit Guavos.

49. CSP 1681-85 no 378 Molesworth to Blathwayt, 25 Sept 1685. no 778 Molesworth to Blathwayt, 17 July 1686; no 824 Edward Randolph to Lords of Trade and Plantations, Boston, 23 Aug 1686; no 897 Molesworth to Blathwayt, 5 Oct 1686

50. CSP no 1,449 Molesworth to Blathwayt, 30 Sept 1687; Captains Yankey and Jacob to Lieutenant Governor Molesworth, Montego Bay, 3 Sept 1687; no 1,476 Lt Governor Molesworth to William Blathwayt, 24 Oct 1687 no 1,477 Captains John Williams (Yankey) and Jacob Everson (Jacob) to Lt Governor Molesworth.; Molesworth to Captains Williams and Everson, St Jago de la Vega, 9 Oct 1687; no 1,624 Governor the Duke of Albemarle, 11 Feb 1688; no 1,705 the Duke of Albemarle to Lords of Trade and Plantations, 16 April 1688; no 1,877 Captain Francis Nicholson, Boston, 31 Aug 1688.

CHAPTER FOUR

A NOTORIOUS RENDEZVOUS: CAYMAN IN THE 'GREAT AGE' OF PIRACY, 1717-1733

The opening decades of the 18th century have been described as the 'great age of piracy' when the return to peace, after decades of war, the resulting shrinkage of naval forces, and the impending destitution of an enormous class of sailors, freebooters and adventurers, combined to produce an unprecedented wave of sea-borne crime. The adventures of Blackbeard and his ilk may have launched a thousand swashbuckling images but as this chapter reveals, this lawless age was rather one of violence and ignominy, as the brutality of pirate tortures was met by the sword and shot of determined naval pursuers and by the gloomy finality of the colonial gibbet.

BLACKBEARD AND THE NEW PROVIDENCE PIRATES

Captain Johnson, the great chronicler of pirate stories, who first published his 'General History' in 1724 and was thus a contemporary of those he featured, is supposed to have gleaned his details of the early and private lives of his subjects from interviews with their confreres, as well as from the transcripts of pirate trials and newspaper reports. The anecdotes related may in some instances be embroidered or romanticised, but, given the difficulty of amassing the evidence of the real men hidden by the images which the pirates themselves were anxious to project, Johnson remains one of the best sources of information for the less well documented lives behind the pirate mythology. A more recent historian of the pirates who roamed the Caribbean Seas in the second decade of the 18th century, has suggested that around three quarters of all of them belonged to two groups.

The first included perhaps that most notorious of all – Blackbeard, and operated from a base on New Providence in the Bahamas. Other members of this group included Bonnet, Vane, and Rackham, together with his female pirate crew. [1]

The Story of Edward Teach
– the man they called 'Blackbeard'

Johnson tells us that Blackbeard, born Edward Teach, was a Bristol man who became a privateer in 1716. He was one of a group of outlaws based in the Bahamas, especially on New Providence, and known to have used Cayman as a stopping-off point. In 1717 Teach sailed from there in a sloop with Captain Benjamin Hornigold, and took a prize of a French ship bound for Martinique. He mounted 40 guns on her, naming her the 'Queen Ann's Revenge'. With this impressive ship under his command, Blackbeard mounted a reign of terror. Among the attacks his crew carried out on smaller vessels, one took place at Grand Cayman. According to Johnson, Blackbeard and his crew captured a small turtler anchored off the island, before sailing on towards Havana and Carolina. [1]

In December 1717, Henry Bostock, a sailor, was aboard his sloop 'Margaret', coming from Porto Rico towards Crab Island, when he had a nasty surprise. Meeting a large ship and a sloop, he was fired on and ordered to board his attackers:

> *Being conducted to the quarter deck to the person that was called*
> *the Captain by the mariners (as he thinks of Capt Teach) he asked*
> *this deponent what he had on board to which this deponent*
> *answered he had cattle and hogs, then the said Capt Tach ordered*
> *his own boat to be hoisted out to go on board and fetch them which*
> *they did (they were four Beeves and about five and thirty hogs) they*
> *took from him besides two thirds of a barrel of gunpowder, five*
> *small arms two cutlaces, his books and instruments and some linen.*

Bostock reported that the ship had 36 guns mounted, and almost 300 men on board. He was kept on the pirate ship for around 8 hours, and before they were freed, two of his men - Edward Salter, a cooper, and Martin Fowler - were kept by the pirates. A third, Robert Bibby from Liverpool joined them voluntarily.

Bostock was struck by the riches he saw on the Queen Anne's Revenge:

> *he saw a great deal of plate on board of them, tankards, cups etc,*
> *particularly one of his men took notice of a very fine cup which they told*
> *him they had taken out of one Captain Taylor whom they had taken*
> *going from Barbados to Jamaica … among other riches he believed they*
> *had much gold dust on board.*

Blackbeard was described by his victim as "a tall spare man with a very black beard which he wore very long". Bostock learnt from the pirate crew that they had already attacked and burnt several other vessels, and that they were headed for Hispaniola to careen and to *"lye in wait for the Spanish Armada that they expected would immediately after Christmas come out of the Havana for Hispaniola and PortoRico with ye money to pay the Garrisons"*.

The sloop, travelling in company with the Queen Anne's Revenge, which mounted ten guns and carried 70 men, was commanded by Major Stede Bonnet, an inhabitant of Barbados. Together, the two were believed to have "committed a great many barbarities". [2]

BLACKBEARD DUELLING

One of the most discussed and illustrated of Caribbean pirates, this stylised image was produced to publicise a play entitled 'Blackbeard or the Captive Princess' written in 1824.

ANECDOTES ABOUT BLACKBEARD

It was said of Blackbeard that:

- he had 14 wives

- instead of waiting for victims to hand over their rings, he just chopped off their fingers.

- if he saw a woman who took his fancy he would take her aboard his ship and have a member of his crew perform a mock marriage service.

- one woman refused to marry him saying he was so smelly she would sooner kiss a pig

- he forced his women to dance by firing pistols at their feet

- his skull is in the Peabody Museum in Salem, Massachusetts.

(Pascall, J. *Pirates and Privateers*, p. 42; Oliver, M. *Blackbeard and his murderous mateys*, p. 27, 34, 36).

In the winter of 1717-18, Blackbeard plundered ships off St Kitts and in the Bay of Honduras. Through his piracy, Blackbeard's fleet grew. In May 1718 the Governor of Bermuda reported that he was in the area of New Providence "in a ship of 36 guns and 300 men, also in company with them a sloop of 12 guns and 115 men and two other ships". When he attacked the 'Protestant Caesar' off the Bay of Honduras, he was in a squadron of five ships flying black and red pirate flags. In the summer, Blackbeard was reported to be travelling in a fleet of four ships, numbering in all around 700 men.

Governors of the American and Caribbean colonies began to express their fear in the face of such a fearsome foe, requesting "*the assistance of a frigate or two to cruse hereabouts upon them for we are continually alarmed and our ships taken to the utter ruin of our trade*". The Governor of South Carolina was particularly concerned, Blackbeard having twice appeared off shore,

> *takeing and plundering all ships that either goe out or come in to this port, about 14 days ago 4 sail of them appeared in sight of the town tooke our pilot boat and afterwards 8 or 9 sail with severall of the best inhabitants of this place on board and then sent me word if I did not imediately send them a chest of medicins they would put every prisoner to death which for there sakes being complied with after plundering them of all they had were sent ashore almost naked.*

Following this incident, the ships moved off to the north, but the Governor was gloomy about prospects given the ubiquity of the ex-privateers, and criticised the policy of offering pardons :

> *Those people are so accustomed to this easy way of living that nothing cann reclaime and most of those that took up with the Proclamation are now return'd to the same imployment which has rather proved an encouragement that anything else, there now being three for one there was before the Proclamation was put out. They are now come to such a head that there is no trading in these parts, it being almost impossible to avoid them and nothing but a consider-able force can reduce them which at first might have been done at an easy charge, had the Govt but rightly appraised what sort of people they generally are and how most of them that first turn'd pirates have formerly lived being such as had always sailed in these parts in privateers and lived in the Bay of Campechia.* [3]

Another of the Bahama-based pirates, Charles Vane, was also terrorising the inhabitants of South Carolina. In October 1718, the Governor reported that two of his ships had taken a slaver from Guinea, and captured four outward bound ships. Feeling bound to attack them, a force comprising two sloops was fitted out to go after the pirates. Unable to find Vane, the pirate hunters stumbled instead, in Cape Feare River, upon Stede Bonnet's sloop and two prizes:

> On seeing our vessells enter the River, they endeavoured to gett out, and in the chase, all the three sloops run aground on some shoals. But that commanded by Capt Masters, in which Col. Rhett was, lay within musqt. shott of the pirate, and the water falling away (it being ebb) she keel'd towards him, which exposed our men very much to their fire, for near six hours, dureing wch. time they were engaged very warmly, untill the water riseing sett our sloops afloat, about an hour before the pirate, when Col. Rhett makeing the signall, and they prepair'd to board him, which the pirate seeing, sent a white flagg, and after some short time, surrender'd, on Coll. Rhett's promising he wou'd interceed for mercy. Wee had killed on board Coll. Rhett 8 men and 14 wounded, of which 4 are since dead, and on board Capt Hall, 2 killed and 6 wounded. The said pirates are now prisoners here, and wee are prepairing for their tryall. This undertaking, besides that it has been a considerable expence to us, will (wee apprehend) very much irretate the pirates who infest this coast in great numbers. [4]

During the course of the action Blackbeard had lost his ship and run two of his sloops aground, marooning 17 crew members on an islet, and leaving them with no means of subsistence. Despite the reversal in their fortunes, this was not to be the end of the group's piracy. In December 1718 the Governor of South Carolina reported that the colonists had been subjected to "further insults" by the pirates: "wee having been blocked up and several ships taken in sight of the town". Bonnet had gone out in a sloop and had been committing further piracies but had since been taken again at South Carolina. Teach kept his pursuers at bay for a time by declaring a desire to reform and settle ashore in Carolina, whilst continuing to commit piracies off the coast of North

Carolina. Captain Ellis, of the 'Lyme', reported that Teach

gave out he designed to be a inhabitant and leave off his piratical life and the more to give a gloss to his designs he marryed there, as soon as I received this advice, I employed a man that was going into North Carolina to inform himself of how the fellow lived and if, after the manner he gave out. I recvd severall accounts from people that came from thence that he did continue in that place insulting and abusing the masters of all trading sloops and taking from them what goods and liquors he pleased and that he might not be called a pyrate, paid such prices to them for their effects as he pleased.

By now, however, time was also running out for Blackbeard. Governor Spotswood of Virginia, finally decided to take action:

Having gained sufficient intelligence of the strength of Tache's crew, and sent for pylots from Carolina, I communicated to the Captains of HM ships of war on this station the project I had formed to extirpate this nest of pyrates. It was found impracticable for the men of war to go into the shallow and difficult channells of that country, and the Captains were unwilling to be at the charge of hyring sloops which they had no orders to do, and must therefore have paid out of their own pocketts, but as they readily consented to furnish men, I undertook the other part of supplying at my own charge sloops and pilots. Accordingly I hyred two sloops and put pilotes on board, and the Captains of HM ships having put 55 men on board under the command of the first Lieutenant of the Pearle and an officer from the Lyme.

At the behest of the Governor of Virginia, the expedition "in quest of ye Pirate Teach" was authorised to offer a reward of £100 for the capture of Blackbeard, and sums ranging between £10 and £40 for pirate crew members. Robert Maynard, a naval officer, recorded in his log book on 17 November 1718 *"this day I recd from Capt Gordon an Order to Command 60 Men out of his Majesties Ships Pearl & Lyme ... in Order to destroy some pyrates, who reside in N Carolina".*

As the Governor later reported, with much satisfaction,

they came up with Tach at Ouacock Inlett on the 22nd of last month, he was on board a sloop wch. carryed 8 guns and very well fitted for fight. As soon as he perceived the King's men intended to board him, he took up a bowl of liquor and calling out to the Officers of the other sloops, drank Damnation to anyone that should give or ask quarter, and then discharged his great guns loaded with partridge shott, wch. killed and wounded 20 of the King's men who lay exposed to his fire without any barricade or other shelter; he resolutely entered the first sloop which boarded him, nor did any one of his men yeild while they were in a condition to fight. His orders were to blow up his own vessell if he should happen to be overcome, and a negro was ready to set fire to the powder, had he not been luckily prevented by a planter forced on board the night before and who lay in the hold of the sloop during the action of the pyrats. [5]

The epic battle which resulted in the slaying of Blackbeard, and the killing and wounding of numbers of men on both sides, was reported, in the log of HMS Lyme, with very little pomp. On Thursday 20 November Captain Ellis wrote *"this day our sloops took the Pirate Teach with the loss of most of his men. Killd and wounded. 17 of our men killd and wounded"*. The Boston News gave the story greater panache, describing how, as Maynard's sloop had drawn near Blackbeard, the pirate had boarded her with 10 of his crew, engaging in vicious hand to hand fighting. Maynard and Teach clashed swords, then, drawing his pistol, Maynard reportedly wounded the tall figure with a shot, but he still stood. Finally, as the paper explained, "a Highlander engaged Teach with his broad sword .. Gave Teach a cut on the neck, Teach saying well done lad; the Highlander replied, 'If it be not well done, I'll do it better'. With that he gave him a second stroke, which cut off his head, laying it flat on his shoulder". By the time Blackbeard fell, he reportedly had 5 shot and 20 cuts in his body.

Teach, along with nine of his crew were killed, and 3 white men and 6 blacks from the pirate ships were taken alive but wounded. His severed head was displayed by Maynard from the bowsprit as he sailed back to claim his reward. [6]

Blackbeard had captured the imagination of his contemporaries. His fearsome appearance and manner was already becoming the stuff of legend. Yet, in two years of piratical attacks, and despite taking booty from around 20 ships, Blackbeard does not seem to have had very rich pickings. Close to the scene of his last battle, 140 bags of cocoa and 10 casks of sugar were recovered from a tent found on shore. These, together with his few personal effects, were taken to Virginia.

Some of Blackbeard's men continued as pirates after his death. In 1724 John Rose-Archer was brought to trial along with several other pirates at Boston, Massachusetts. John Masters gave evidence at the trial that he had, in October 1723 been taken by the pirates, on a vessel where Rose Archer was serving as quarter master.

Archer was already trading on the notoriety of his former commander. In April 1724 William Lancy was taken by pirates and Archer had been one of those who came on board his schooner armed with a sword or cutlass. Archer told him he was one of Teach's men and went into South Carolina upon the Act of Grace. John Archer, at his trial, stated however that he was a forced man. Questioned as to how he had come to be a pirate quarter master, he stated that the Company, thinking him the fittest, had chosen him as such. On 2nd June 1724 the 27 year old John Rose Archer was hanged on Bird Island in Boston harbour and his body exhibited on a gibbet. [7]

Stede Bonnet, Charles Vane, and Calico Jack Rackham

Blackbeard's one time pirate consort, Major Stede Bonnet was reputedly from an unusual background for an outlaw. Retired from the army, he had become a respectable plantation owner in Barbados. Depicted as stout, clean-shaven and dressed in wig and gentlemen's dress, he cut an unlikely figure as a pirate. It is suggested that he turned to piracy from a sense of adventure, joining Blackbeard's fleet in 1717. Captured by the Henry and the

Sea Nymph, who were out hunting for Charles Vane in 1718, Bonnet continued his piracy for a while longer, before being recaptured and hung in the same year. [8]

CHARLES VANE

STEDE BONNET

Charles Vane was a former mariner from Port Royal, Jamaica. During his short piratical career, he commanded a six gun sloop, and a twelve gun brigantine, which carried a crew of 90 men. [9]

The year 1718 was the apogee of Vane's career. In March, commanding two sloops, Vane seized "*the John and Elizabeth, taking several hundred Spanish pieces of eight and diverse goods on board her, which was heading from St Augustine to the Island of Providence, taking lading, tackle, furniture and apparel worth 1,000 pounds*". In May, the Governor of Bermuda reported him to be cruising in the 'Ranger', a sloop of 6 guns and with 60 men. On 14th April, Samuel Cooper was on board the 'Diamond' sloop at Rum Key when Vane attacked, taking their money, a slave, cutting the mast and bowspritt, and brutalising the crew. It was said that up to 12 other vessels, at least 7 of them from Bermuda, were treated in the same way. The Bermudians were particularly targeted, according to Cooper, in revenge for the detention of one of their number, Thomas Brown. Brown reportedly *"had subscriptions of hands to the number of 70 in order to go out under his command upon the account of piracy and would give no quarters to Bermudians"*. Edward North deponed likewise that Vane's men

> *took from him 17 pistoles and an half (being all the money that was on board) 10 ounces of Ambergreece or thereabouts, one negro man and several necessaryes, and barbarously treated the deponent with all his company by beating them and using other cruelties, particularly to one, who they bound hands and feet and ty'd (upon his back) down to the bowspritt with matches to his eyes burning and a pistol loaded with the muzzle into his mouth, thereby to oblige him to confess what money was on board.* [10]

Joseph Besea, also of Bermuda, was unlucky enough to chance upon Vane, five days after that incident, near Crooked Island in the Bahamas. Lewis Middleton, commander of the sloop 'Fortune', testified around the same time that he had picked up three men who had been turned adrift by the pirates. Nathaniel Catling, aboard the Diamond sloop in the Bahamas when he met Vane, had a particular grievance, claiming that he had been

> *hang'd up by the neck untill (as he was afterwards inform'd) they thought he was Dead, and then let him down upon the Deck and one of them perceiving he began to revive cut him with a cutlass over his collar bone and would have continued the same till he had murdered this deponent had not one of their own gang contradicted it, being (as he said) too great a cruelty).*

Vane's victims testified to the violence of his utterances, in particular his contempt for authority figures. They reported his use of what were for the time treasonable and shocking expressions: 'curse the King and all the Higher Powers', 'Damn the Governour' and 'Damnation to King George'.

Vane was smoked out of his lair on New Providence, Bahamas, by the arrival of Woodes Rogers, the new Governor, in July 1718. The Governor, given instructions to act against the privateers, had been preceded by his reputation, for he was greeted, on arriving at the harbour of the island by

> *a French ship (that was taken by the pirates of 22 guns) burning in the harbour which we were told was set on fire to drive out HMS the Rose who got in too eagerly the evening before me, and cut her cables and run out in the night for fear of being burnt, by one Charles Vane who command'd the pirates and at ours and HMS the Milford's near approach the next morning they finding it impossible to escape us, he with about 90 men fled away in a sloop wearing the black flag, and fir'd guns of defiance when they perceiv'd their sloop out sayl'd the two that I sent to chase them hence.*

Benjamin Hornigold, himself a former privateer who had sailed with Blackbeard, having now been pardoned, was recruited by Woodes Rogers to deal with Vane:

> *I got a sloop fitted under the command of Capt Hornygold to send and view them and bring me an accot. what they were, in the mean time I keep a very strick't watch for fear of any surprize, and not hearing from Capt. Hornigold I was afraid he was either taken by Vaine or begun his old practice of pirating again, wch. was the general opinion here in his absence, but to my great satisfaction he return'd in about three weeks having lain most of that time concealed and viewing of Vaine the Pirate in order to surprize him or some of his men that they expected would be near them in their boats, but tho they failed in this Capt. Hornygold brought with.him a sloop of this place, that got leave from me to go out a turtling but had been trading wth. Vaine who had then with him two ships and a brigantine, his sloop that he escaped hence in being runaway with by another set of new pirates, the two ships he took coming out of Carolina one of 400 and the other of 200 tons loaded with rice, pitch and tarr and skins bound for London, the Neptune, Captain King being the largest he sunk and the Emperours Capt Arnold Gowers he left without doing her any damage except taking away their provisions.*

Woodes Rogers arrested the merchant known to have been trading
with Vane, and despite "*having not yet a power to make an example
of them here he remains in irons to be sent home to England by the
next ship*". Vane continued to set himself at defiance against
Rogers, who recorded:

> *This Vaine had the impudence to send me word that he designs to
> burn my guardship and visit me very soon to return the affront, I
> gave him on my arrival in sending two sloops after him instead of
> answering the letter he sent me. He expects soon to joyne Majr
> Bonnet or some other pirate, and then I am to be attack'd by them.*

Rogers, however, strengthening the defences of New Providence,
declared himself "*not concern'd at his threats. Capt. Hornygold
having proved honest, and disobliged his old friends by seazing
this vessel it devides the people here and makes me stronger than
I expected*". [11]

Vane's threats against the Governor of New Providence were
never to be acted out. He was voted out of the command of his
ship in November 1718, his crew accusing him of cowardice in
failing to attack a potential French prize, appointing the
quartermaster in his place. Vane and 16 of the men were put on
board a small sloop, with provisions and ammunition to provide
for themselves. Vane's luck was about to run out, however. In
February 1719, cruising south of Jamaica, his sloop was caught in a
storm, and he was swept to a deserted islet in the Bay of Honduras.
The sloop was destroyed, and most of the crew were killed. Vane
survived, helped by local fishermen who came to the islet to catch
turtles. The pirate was eventually rescued, only to be taken to
Jamaica for trial. [12]

The Vice Admiralty Court was convened at Spanish Town in
Jamaica on 22 March 1720. Among the numerous accusations
ranged against Vane were the following:

> *taking the John and Elizabeth on 29 March, and of having on 17
> April 1 league from Crooked Island having taken a merchant sloop
> named the Betty, stealing goods worth 200 pounds, and on 22*

April of having 3 leagues from Crooked Island, take a merchant
sloop called the Fortune and steal goods worth 150 pounds, on 23
May 1718 4 leagues off Crooked Island did shoot at and take a mer-
chant sloop called the Richard and John and steal goods worth 200
pounds, that on 23 Oct 1718, 2 leagues from Long Island did take
Endeavour a brigantine, and steal 250 worth of goods, that on 16
Dec 1718 at the Bay of Honduras did take a merchant sloop called
the Pearl stealing goods worth 100 pounds.

Charles Vane said nothing in his defence, and was found guilty of
piracy and sentenced to bc hanged. He was executed at Gallows Point
in Port Royal and his body was exhibited on a gibbet at Gun Key.
Robert Deal, one of his crew had been tried earlier, on 18 January
1720, and despite pleading that he was a 'forced man', was found
guilty and likewise executed. [13]

It was very satisfactory for the Governor to note, that within the space
of a few months, Vane and his former quartermaster, Calico Jack
Rackham were both executed: *"two notorious Comanders of Pirate*
Vessells suffered and died most profligate impudent villains".

Probably a mariner by trade, in 1718 John Rackham was already
well into his career of piracy, serving as quartermaster in a crew
commanded by Charles Vane. He no doubt participated in the plunder
of a ship off South Carolina in that year and was probably on board in
October when Vane's 12 gun pirate brigantine captured the
'Endeavour', commanded by John Shattock, hoisting a black flag and
a firing at its prey. Shattock later reported that he had been beaten by
the pirates in an effort to obtain his money, but that he was allowed to
depart after his vessel had been stripped of valuables. On 23
November 1718 Vane's men attacked a French warship but, being
repulsed, the pirates reportedly began to quarrel amongst
themselves. The result was that pirate chief, Vane, one of his officers,
Robert Deal, and 15 others were offloaded onto a smaller sloop,
equipped with food and ammunition. Rackham now assumed
command of the larger sloop in place of Vane. Continuing towards
the Caribbean islands, the pirates plundered 2 or 3 more vessels,
including a Madeiran, bound for Jamaica. [14]

Rackham was now a fully fledged pirate captain and perhaps from this time dates his reputation for womanising. He is reported to have kept a harem of mistresses on the coast of Cuba. In fact, Rackham seems to have tired of pirating for a time, opting to sail to New Providence in the Bahamas around May 1719, where the Governor was offering a royal pardon to pirates. He settled there for a while until the difficulties arising from his involvement with a married woman, Anne Bonny, led to his return to the old ways— stealing a ship and taking to the high seas.

'CALICO JACK'

There is no evidence of 'Calico Jack' Rackham torturing or murdering his victims as was the case with some of his fellow marauders, including Vane.

Rackham operated a relatively small sloop, returning captured vessels to their crew when he had finished looting, and usually restricting his attacks to local trading vessels and fishing boats

Rackham was holed up at a cove on the Cuban coast when an incident occurred which revealed his particular brand of daring. A Spanish ship with an English prize, seeing his sloop, came in to the shore to capture him. Rackham seemed to be boxed in, with little prospect of escape. At dead of night, however, Rackham lowered a small boat and, with his crew, rowed round the island to the unsuspecting English prize which he boarded – overcoming the prize crew and taking her out to sea. When the Spanish crew commenced attacking the pirate sloop at daylight, they found her empty, and their own prize made off with!

The activities of John Rackham in the later months of 1720 are known in greater detail as a result of evidence later given against him. On 3rd September he captured several fishing boats near Harbour Island and by early October was off the island of Hispaniola where he seized two merchant sloops and got away with goods worth £1,000. Here also, he accosted two Frenchmen hunting close to shore and forced them to come aboard. No doubt he was to regret this kidnap, as the men would prove to be important witnesses against him. In their statements, Peter Cornelian and John Besneck, the Frenchmen, claimed that they were

> *taken off the Shoar of the Island of Hispaniola in America, (as they were hunting wild Hog) in a Canoa or Pettiago, and afterwards ... put on Board a Sloop at Sea, commanded by one Rackam, ... and forced by him and his Crew to go with them.*

By the 19th of October Rackam's sloop was located off Port Maria Bay in Jamaica where he shot at and took a schooner. Thomas Spenlow, the vessel's master, recorded later that the pirates had

> *fired a small Arm at him; whereupon he brought to, being afraid, and then the Sloops Crew boarded him, and took him; and took out of his said Scooner, 50 Rolls of Tobacco, and 9 bags of Piemento, and kept him in their Custody about 48 hours, and then let him .... depart.* [15]

Spenlow was still with the pirates when, the next day, they attacked another sloop off Dry Harbour Bay in Jamaica, "*firing several great Guns at her, and afterwards boarded her, and took her, and carried her with them to Sea*". This was, however, to be the last of Rackam's exploits, for, still with the second sloop in his possession, he stopped off at Negril-point at the West end of Jamaica. Nine sailors, who claimed to be on a turtling expedition, were hailed by Rackham on the 22nd October there. John Eaton, one of the nine, said that "*they saw a sloop with a white pendant, coming towards them; upon which they took their arms, and hid themselves in the bushes, that one of the prisoners, afterwards, hailed the sloop, who answer'd, they were Englishmen, and desired them all to come on board, and drink a bowl of punch; which they at first refused, but afterwards, with much persuasion, they went on board in the sloop's canoe"*. John Besneck, who had earlier been captured by Rackam's men and was still on board, offered his own interpretation of their conduct. He asserted that the 9 mariners "brought guns, and cutlasses, on board with them: that they drank together with the pirates crew".

As the pirates and their guests drank, and strolled on the decks, they were themselves sighted and approached. The pursuer was Captain Jonathan Barnet, commissioned in 1715 by the Governor of Jamaica, with instructions "by force of arms to seize, take and apprehend all pyratical ships and vessels with their commander, officers and crew", and to bring any captives to Port Royal. The pirate sloop fired on Barnet's vessel, the 'Tyger', prompting him to give chase.

James Spatchears described what happened next:

> *about Ten a Clock at Night [Barnet's vessel] came up with [the pirate sloop], and hailed her; whereto some of the said Sloop's Company answer'd John Rackam From Cuba; then Barnet bid him strike immediately, to the King of England's Colours; upon which some Body answer'd from the said Sloop .. That they would strike no Strikes, and immediately fired a Swivil Gun at Barnet's Sloop; whereupon Barnet order'd his Men to fire a Broad-side and Volley of Small-shot at the said Sloop, which they did, and carried away the Enemy Sloop's Boom, and then they called to Barnet for Quarter, which he gave them, and afterwards took the said Sloop and Dillon's Sloop, which they had before taken, and was then in their custody, and put all the Men ashoar at Davis's Cove on the Island of Jamaica, and delivered them to Major Richard James (a Militia Officer) who procured a Guard, in order to carry them to Spanish-Town Gaol.*

This was to be the end of Rackham's days as a pirate. And the hapless sailors who had been aboard such a short while, were to pay heavily for their drink. The French witnesses declared that as the pirate sloop was attacked, the sailors left the deck, but some later helped to row the sloop, in an endeavour to escape from Captain Barnet. John Eaton spoke for them all, when called to account for their actions, saying: "*they had been but a short time on board when Capt Barnet's Sloop heaved in sight; that Rackam ordered the[m] to help to weight the sloop's anchor immediately, which they all refus'd; That Rackam used violent means to oblige them; and that when Captain Barnet came up with them, they all readily and willingly surrendered themselves*". Despite the mitigating circumstances, the men, along with Rackham and his crew, were seized as pirates. It was evidently as lethal to consort with pirates, as it was to be a pirate oneself.

After their capture, Rackham and 8 of his men were tried at Spanish Town, Jamaica in November 1720. Sir Nicholas Lawes, the Governor of Jamaica, himself presided over the court. The men were charged with four counts of "*Piracies, Felonies and Robberies, committed by them on the high Sea, and within the Jurisdiction of this Court*" between September and October 1719. They all pleaded Not Guilty. After hearing witnesses, the Commissioners unanimously agreed that the prisoners were guilty of two of the four charges, and the Governor pronounced sentence:

> *You John Rackam, George Fetherston, Richard Corner, John Davies, John Howell, Patrick Carty, Thomas Earl, James Dobbin and Noah Harwood, are to go from hence to the Place from whence you came, and from thence to the Place of Execution; where you shall severally be hanged by the Neck, till you are severally Dead. And may God ... be merciful to every one of your Souls*".

On Friday 18th November 1720 Captain John Rackham and four of his men were executed at Gallows Point in Port Royal. The bodies were afterwards hung on gibbets in chains, to serve as "*a publick Example, and to terrify others from such-like evil Practices*".

The sandy cay off Port Royal where Rackham's body hung for all to see is now named after him. The next day, Noah Harwood, James Dobbin, Patrick Carty and Thomas Earl were executed at the town of Kingston. An exultant Jamaican Governor reported home: *"Rackum the pirate and ten more have been tried and executed which I hope in time will have a good effect"*. [16]

On the 24th January, the hapless sailors who had joined Rackham's sloop shortly before it was captured were also tried for piracy. Despite their protestations of innocence, they too, were pronounced guilty. Eaton, Quick and Baker were executed at Gallows Point, Port Royal on Friday 17 February, and the next day Cole, Howard and Palmer were hung at Kingston. A sorry spectacle had been made of all who joined Rackham, from the hardened pirates to the hangers-on.

At a separate trial, held on 28th November, two of Rackham's crew members, also found guilty of piracy, sensationally escaped death. They were women, Anne Bonny and Mary Read, whose extraordinary life-stories, and whose exploits alongside the colourful Calico Jack, helped to make him one of the most famous of the outlaws of his day.

Anne Bonny was reputedly born in Ireland, the illegitimate daughter of an attorney at law. It was said that her parents had quarrelled and separated, following her father's affair with a household maid. The lawyer wished to have the daughter of this liaison by his side. He accordingly dressed the little girl in boy's clothes, pretending to be training the youngster as a clerk. When his ex-wife revealed the scandal, the attorney decided to move abroad, and left for Carolina with his mistress and their daughter, Anne. Later, however, Anne married a penniless mariner, enraging her father, who threw her out. The Bonnys then went to New Providence in the Bahamas. [17]

It was here that John Rackham reportedly met Anne Bonny, he frequenting, like her, the seaside taverns. Mutually infatuated, the couple contrived a plan to obtain consent to a deed of separation from Anne's husband. The Bahamian Governor, Woodes Rogers, was incensed by what he considered to be lewd and immoral conduct—he threatened to have Anne publicly flogged instead. Elopement was a better option, and once again donning men's attire, Mrs Bonny took to the sea with her pirate paramour.

ANNE BONNY

Anne Bonny was evidently an active member of Rackham's crew, and well adapted to pirate life. The Frenchmen kidnapped at Hispaniola described Anne as *"very active on Board, and willing to do anything ... Ann Bonny handed gun powder to the men"*. She dressed as a man or woman as the occasion required.

Thomas Dillon, whose sloop was attacked off Jamaica on 20 October 1720, also reported seeing Anne Bonny on board Rackham's sloop, noting that she cursed as well as any of the male pirates, and held a gun in her hand. Other eye-witnesses claimed that the women made a better show of fighting off their pursuers than the male crew members. [18]

The spirit of Anne Bonny is best shown by the last interview she allegedly had with John Rackham. Permitted to visit him on the day of his execution. She is said to have told Calico Jack *"that she was sorry to see him there, but if he had fought like a Man, he need not have been hang'd like a Dog"*. Anne Bonny was tried, shortly after her lover, for the same crimes. She escaped execution by virtue of another pregnancy, and some say was returned to Carolina following her father's intercession with well-placed merchants of the colony.

MARY READ

Mary reportedly became a pirate after a ship in which she was travelling—dressed as a man—was captured by them.

Why Mary Read came to be sailing the seas in male attire is a story almost too strange to be true—if we are to believe the facts unearthed by Captain Johnson. Like Anne Bonny, Mary Read was illegitimate—the second child of a married woman whose husband had gone away to sea and never returned. When the first, legitimate son died, the mother decided to disguise her daughter in boy's clothes, to pass her off as that son in order to gain support from her mother-in-law. When a crown a week was indeed offered to maintain the 'boy', Mary was obliged to continue in the disguise. At the age of 13 she obtained a job as a 'footman' in a French household. Now grown bold and strong, Mary ran away from this drudgery, first enlisting on a man-of-war, and later serving as an army cadet in Flanders. [19]

By all accounts, Mary was a good soldier, even distinguishing herself for her bravery in battle. Falling in love with a fellow soldier, of Flemish origin, she revealed herself to be a woman, and became his mistress. The couple eventually married, left the army and took on a public house, 'The Three Horse Shoes', at Breda, with a largely military clientele. Sadly, her husband died and, after the Peace of 1697, the army moved away. Mary was left without an income and decided to resume her masculine disguise. She again enlisted as a soldier, serving in a regiment of foot, before embarking on a merchant ship bound for the West Indies. Its capture threw her into the path of pirates, and before long she had joined Rackham's gang.

There is some evidence that Mary Read had embarked on a piratical way of life, or at least associated with pirates before 1709, as her name figures on a petition sent to Queen Anne in that year by the wives and relatives of Madagascar and West Indies based 'Pirates and Buccaneers', pleading for a royal pardon. Their request was eventually granted in 1717.

Initially undiscovered as a man by any of Rackham's crew, Mary Read was obliged to reveal her disguise to Anne Bonny, when the latter, attracted by the smooth-faced new recruit, attempted to seduce her! Rackham, becoming jealous of his lover's interest in the young 'boy', was also let into the secret.

Following the theft of the 'William' in August 1720, Captain Woodes Rogers, the Governor of the Bahamas, also seemed well aware of the identities of the culprits, for on 5 September he issued a proclamation listing Rackham, Bonny and Mary Read by name and declaring them "Pirates and Enemies to the Crown of Great Britain".

After their capture, Mary Read and Anne Bonny were taken with Rackham and the others to Jamaica, and tried - separately from the men - on Monday 28th November 1720. Described as spinsters, "late of the island of Providence", the women were accused of four counts of piracy between September and October of the same year. On their pleading not guilty, a number of witnesses were called to give evidence.

Dorothy Thomas, whose canoe, stocked with provisions, had been intercepted by the pirates off the north coast of Jamaica, described Anne and Mary as clothed in

> *Mens Jackets, and long Trouzers, and Handkerchiefs tied about their Heads; and that each of them had a Machet and Pistol in their Hands, and cursed and swore at the Men, to murder the Deponent; and that they should kill her, to prevent her coming against them; ..., That the Reason of her knowing and believing them to be Women then was, by the largeness of their Breasts.*

Another witness, Thomas Dillon, whose sloop had been seized while at Dry Harbour, in Jamaica, described both women as being *"very profligate, cursing and swearing much, and very ready and willing to do any Thing on board"*.

OLD PIRATE SONG ATTRIBUTED TO ANNE BONNY:

Drain, drain the bowl,
each fearless soul,
Let the world wag as it will,
Let the heavens growl,
the devil howl,
Drain, drain the bowl
and fill!

Anne Bonny fighting a man

The women proffered no witnesses or evidence of their own and were accordingly found guilty and sentenced to death. Fortunately for the women, both were then pregnant, and having announced this to the court, their sentences were revoked. This did not save Mary Read: she died of fever shortly afterwards and was buried in the parish of St. Catherine's in Jamaica, on 28 April 1721. [20]

THE CAYMAN PACT OF 1721:
GEORGE LOWTHER AND EDWARD LOW

The extraordinary successes of the 17th century privateers had occurred when they were able to rendezvous and combine forces. Pirates, too, whose crews linked up and created a spirit of camaraderie, could find strength in numbers and set in course a chain of attacks which sowed terror in the hearts of humble settlers and wealthy merchants alike. When Edward Low met up with George Lowther at West Bay on Grand Cayman in 1721, their combined crews created one of the most successful brotherhoods of the 'great age' of piracy.

George Lowther and Edward Low were both ex-mariners. Lowther had worked as a second mate in the 'Gambia Castle', a ship of the Royal African Company. Low, born in Westminster, had worked as a seaman, spending some time at a rigging house in Boston, New England.

Both were involved in violent disagreements and revolts which set them on a course of piracy. Aboard the 'Gambia Castle', in May 1721, off the coast of Africa, Lowther led a mutiny, while Low, after an altercation with his employers, boarded a sloop bound for the Bay of Honduras where he took charge of a boat employed in cutting log wood. At some point, tiring of the work, Low and 12 companions decided to seize a small boat and set off on their own account. [21]

Lowther, taking over the 'Gambia Castle', renamed it the 'Delivery' and, manning it with 50 of the mariners, hoisted black colours and cruised the Caribbean. Low and his 12 companions, also ran up a pirate flag for themselves. They decided to make for Grand Cayman, where they hoped to fit up their boat and equip themselves as best they could as pirates.

Stopping at Grand Cayman for water, Lowther came across the small vessel with its 13 hands, anchored near a white sand beach, captained by Edward Low. He invited them to join him, offering Low the position of lieutenant. Low's vessel was accordingly abandoned and sunk. Its wreck presumably lies somewhere off Cayman to this day.

In the second half of 1721 and the first half of 1722 the pirates were reported to have carried out a number of attacks. Captain George Roberts (whose book, published in 1726, is believed by some to be entirely fictitious) claimed to have been taken prisoner by Edward Low who was travelling in a squadron of pirate ships, off the Cape Verde islands, around September 1721. He described at length the prodigious amount of eating, and particularly drinking which took place on board Low's vessel.

In June 1722 when Philip Ashton was among a number of men captured by the pirate in the harbour of Port Rossoway, he was terrified to have a pistol put to his head. Low would only take men, Ashton stated, if they were unmarried, apparently because he had himself a child in Boston, although his wife was long since dead. Ashton was horrified by the comportment of the men in whose company he found himself, describing them as

> a vile crew of miscreants, to whom it was a sport to do mischief, were prodigious drinking, monstrous cursing and swearing, hideous blasphemies, and open defiance of Heaven, and contempt of hell itself, was the constant employment. [22]

In August 1722 Low's brigantine was caught up in a hurricane as he was heading for the Leeward Islands in the Caribbean. Struggling against huge waves, the crew jettisoned most of their guns and provisions in an effort to lighten the ship. Lowther led an attack on the 'Amy' off South Carolina, which left him with several injured men. A period of recuperation followed, as the pirates spent the winter in the woods of North Carolina, hunting cattle and hogs by day, and retiring to tents and huts at night.

In March 1723 Low cunningly lured a Spanish merchant ship in the Bay of Honduras to draw close, by hoisting that nation's flag, and then raising the black ensign, before firing on, and boarding her. His quartermaster Nicholas Lewis later testified that the pirate captain killed 45 Spaniards in the cold blooded attack. His sadistic cruelty to his captives was also in evidence, shortly before this incident when he captured a homeward-bound Portuguese ship. The captain dangled his hoard of gold, amounting to 11,000 moydores from the cabin window, cutting it loose and allowing it to fall into the sea, rather than let it fall into Low's hands. In retaliation, as Lewis related, "Lowe cutt off the said Master's lipps and broyl'd them before his face", before murdering the entire crew numbering 32 persons. Asking for a special Proclamation, offering a reward to anyone that could capture Low alive or dead, the Governor of St Christopher opined that "a greater monster never infested the seas". [23]

The pirate captain was soon to meet his nemesis, however. Captain Solgard, who commanded HMS Greyhound, located Low's two sloops, the 'Fortune', and 'Ranger', off Long Island on 10 June 1723. Making as if to head away from the pirates, he encouraged them to chase after the Greyhound. Clearing his ship for action, he allowed the sloops to draw close enough to unleash a volley of shot upon them. During an 8 hour battle, one sloop surrendered, and Low was obliged to flee. Of the captured pirates, 23 were hanged at Newport Harbour on 19 July 1723. Reporting the incident, the Governor of New York noted that Low's sloop had "seem'd much shattered,", and that Solgard, having brought in the one sloop,

> *immediately went out in quest of [her], which he writes me word, he has intelligence by which he believes he shall find her to the eastward of Boston. This blow, with what they received from Captain Ogle will I hope clear the seas of those accomplished villains. These last have been remarkably cruel, and have done vast damage in the West Indies.* 24

In September 1723, George Lowther and his men attacked the 'Princes Galley', which had a cargo of African slaves on board, off Barbados. The ship attempted to escape, but could not flee the pirates, who boarded her. In the words of John Wickstead, her 45 year old commander and his crew:

> *the said pirates detained them all the next day during which time they ransackt and plundered the said ship and put lighted matches between the fingers of the deponents Goldsmith Blowers and John Crawford to make or force them to discover where the gold was and thereupon the said pirates took away some gold being about 54 ounces or thereabouts and their gun powder the remnant of the cargo and small arms with two*

*quarter deck guns and two swivell guns with the gunners and
boatswains stores, the ship colours and several things more that the
said pirates thought fit or were for their purpose and these deponents
say that the said pirates detained by force William Gibbons surgeons
mate and James Sedgwick carpenters mate of the said ship, but that
Abraham Crane, Henry Wynn, Robert Corp, Richard Hardwell and
William Churchill did as these deponants believe goe with the said
pirates voluntarily and these deponents further say that the said
pirate sloop was commanded by one George Lowther having about
eight guns mounted and about 30 men more or less ... the said
pirates took away from them 14 negroes, 13 of which belonged to the
cargo, and the other a privilege slave.* [25]

The sailors who had left the employ of Wickstead to join Lowther's
gang, must have rued their decision. Tried for piracy at St
Christopher's on 11th March 1724, they were charged, that they did

*betray the Trust reposed in them and feloniously and piratically
turn Pirates and Rebells and voluntarily joyn and go with and
adhere unto the said George Lowther and other the Pirates in the
said Sloop ... and did on the fifth day of October ... attack and fight
against a certain sloop called the Eagle of Barbadoes*

Robert Corp did not deny the charge, although Henry Wynn, for his
part, pleaded not guilty. Their former shipmates on the 'Princes
Galley' testified against them. Sedgwick and Gibbons, who had
been forced to join Lowther's men, deposed that they had, on the
17th September, seen the accused "*voluntarily sign a Paper which
the said Pirates called their Articles of Regulation*". Corp, Wynn,
and several other pirates were all sentenced to be hanged, the court
deciding they should be executed on Friday 20th March. However,
the judges requested the Governor that

*Robert Corp and Henry Wynn be recommended to his Excellency
as objects of his Majesty's mercy, it not appearing that they had
ever acted any piracys after they consented to associate themselves
to the pirates, and as they were very young, it's uncertain how far
the apprehension of ill usage might prevail over their fears to gain
their consent".* [26]

GEORGE LOWTHER

After his attack on the 'Princes Galley', Lowther retreated to the island of Blanco, in October 1723, to careen his ship.

Walter Moor, captain of the *Eagle*, spotted Lowther's craft as the ship was being careened on Blanco:

> *when this Deponent came near the said Sloop, he was obliged to highst his Colours and fir a Gunn at the Head of the other Sloop, to oblige her to show her Colours, and She answered with highsting a Saint Georges Flagg at the Topmast head, and fired at this Deponents Sloop Eagle, and when they found this Deponent with his Crew was resolved to board the said Sloop, they Cutt their Cables and hawld their Stern on Shore, which obliged this Deponent to come to an Anchor a thawrt their harse, where he Engaged them untill they called for Quarters and Struck; at which time George Lowther who was the Captain on board the saide Pirates with about tenn or twelve of his Crew made their Escape out of the Cabbin Windows And then this Deponent gott the Sloop off and Secured her and went on Shore with Twenty five Men, where they remained five days and nights in pursuit of the said Lowther and Company, and could not retake more than five of them.*

Moor called off the hunt, and left with his prize, but a second sloop was later sent back to the island, with a crew of 25, to search for the remainder of Lowther's men. Four more of the pirates were taken but Lowther himself was "found dead with his Pistoll busted by his side". The captives were tried at St Kitts on 11 March 1724 and several were hanged a week later.

Low meanwhile was off the coast of Africa in September 1723, where he captured a group of coloured Portuguese fishermen from the island of San Antonio near Cape Verde. They were put aboard Captain Peares' Bristol sloop, the Thomas and Jane to be sold as slaves. Captain Baines of Barbados purchased some of them at St Lucia, from where he brought them to his island. The Governor of Barbados was disposed to help them: they having appealed to him as 'freemen and Christians'. He noted that even if they were slaves, they would have to be treated as 'piratical goods'. A month later, Henry Hunt, master of the 'Delight' galley, and his chief mate Thomas Blackson were also captured by Low's ship, the 'Fortune' off the coast of Africa. The men declared that Low who mounted 28 guns and had 80 men with him, took 15 of their crew with him, including a carpenter, a cooper, and even their cook. [27]

GEORGE LOW

Low met an appropriate end. Reportedly set adrift by his own men, he was picked up by a French boat from Martinique, and was summarily hanged.

A PIRATE WRECK AND PIRATE SETTLERS ON GRAND CAYMAN, 1722

The piratical career of Captain Anstis is believed to date from 1718, when he and five others aboard the 'Buck' at Providence conspired to take to piracy. They fell in with notorious pirate Bartholomew Roberts who was involved in the capture of the 'Morning Star' ship and the 'Good Fortune' brigantine. In April 1721 Anstis was in command of the 'Good Fortune', sailing with Roberts for the African coast, when, some 400 leagues off the mainland, Anstis and his crew voted to leave Roberts, departing in the middle of the night.

In June, with Anstis still captaining the 'Good Fortune', now mounting 16 guns and commanding a pirate force of 60 whites and 19 negroes, the crew captured the 'Hamilton', a Bristol ship, off Jamaica. Samuel Pitt, the mate, and 6 others managed to make their way from Havana to the Bahamas in a longboat and raised the alarm. The second mate and 12 sailors had been forced to go with the pirates. [28]

Subsequently, Anstis' crew, many of whom were ex-mariners of the 'Morning Star' and 'Good Fortune' decided to represent themselves as having been forced into their present way of life by Roberts, and petitioned the Governor of Jamaica for a pardon. While they were waiting to learn their fate, Jones, former boatswain on the 'Good Fortune', proposed as a place of retreat, an uninhabited island near Cuba, which he knew from his days of privateering against the Spaniards. [29]

The men stayed here for about 9 months, living on fish and turtle meat which was plentiful on the coasts. They passed their time in dancing and other diversions, even appointing a mock Court to try one another for piracy taking turns to play the roles of accused and accusers. The 'judge' would sit in a tree with a dirty tarpaulin hung over his shoulders for a robe, wearing a yarn cap and a large pair of spectacles upon his nose. His 'officers' would be in attendance below with crows and handspikes. The judge's mock summing up reveals the pirates' anti-establishment attitudes and their contempt for the justice system.

THOMAS ANSTIS' MEN HOLD A MOCK TRIAL

The judge's summing up:

You must suffer for three reasons; first, because it is not fit I should sit here as judge and nobody be hanged; secondly, you must be hanged because you have a damned hanging look; and thirdly, you must be hanged because I am hungry; for know, Sirrah, that 'tis a custom that whenever the judge's dinner is ready before the trial is over, the prisoner is to be hanged of course. There's Law for you, ye dog! So take him away, gaoler. [30]

In August 1722 the pirates left their retreat to find out if their petition had had an effect, but without a favourable reply set out to return to the island. The next day, "*by intolerable neglect, they ran the 'Morning Star' aground at Grand Cayman and wrecked her*". Their brigantine hauled off in time and so weathered the island. The next day Captain Anstis found that most of the crew had safely made it ashore. Anchoring, he succeeded in getting the Captain, Fenn, and Philips, the carpenter and a few others aboard the brigantine, when two men-of-war, the 'Hector' and 'Adventure', sighted them. The pirates hastily rowed back to Grand Cayman but the 'Hector' landed her men on the island and captured 40 of the them. These men then asserted, by way of defence, that they had themselves been the pirates' prisoners. Others hid in the woods and were not found. It is therefore possible that some of Anstis' crew

remained on Grand Cayman indefinitely. Another four, including
George Bradley the master, got off the island by surrendering to a
Bermuda sloop. They may well have been the 'four pyrates' who
arrived on Bermuda "from an island called the Camanos" in May 1723.
The Governor deprecated the "correspondence betwixt the pyrates and
those people that go from hence to those islands". [31]

After this untoward encounter with the notorious reefs off Grand
Cayman, Thomas Anstis went on to accomplish further acts of piracy
before being unceremoniously shot by his own men following a quarrel.

A PIRATE DUEL ON CAYMAN, 1723

Welshman John Evans, formerly master of a sloop belonging to Nevis,
sailed to Jamaica as mate after losing his job. In September 1722, he
and a few others rowed out of Port Royal in a canoe. Deciding that they
needed at bigger boat, at Duns Hole Jamaica, they found a small sloop
at anchor, belonging to Bermuda. They mounted 4 guns on the sloop,
called her the 'Scourer' and sailed in her to Hispaniola, where they took
a Spanish sloop which proved to be a rich prize.

Heading for the Windward Islands, they then plundered the 'Dove',
which was making for Jamaica from New England. On January 11
1723, near the island of Deseada, they took another prize. The pirates
then went to Grand Cayman, intending to careen their sloop there, when
an unhappy incident put an end to their illegal activities. The boatswain
and the captain having previously quarrelled, decided to fight a duel at
the next land they came to. On arrival at Grand Cayman, a further
dispute ensued and Evans was shot through the head by the boatswain,
who immediately left the ship and swam to shore. It is believed that
Boatswain Bay, on Grand Cayman, is named after this officer. The rest
of the pirates sent a boat after him while they deliberated about his
punishment. Presumably demoralised by the Captain's death the
company decided to break up and went ashore at Cayman, reportedly
sharing £9,000 of booty between 30 crew members. [32] It is believed

that at least four of them, who were not voluntary pirates, but forced men, decided to settle permanently on Cayman. Their names were William Porter, Joseph Hyndes, James Moore and Robert Saunders. [33]

A CAYMAN PIRATE COMPANY

Captain Thomas Howard was a lighterman on the River Thames, as his father had been before him. After the latter's death, however, he squandered the family inheritance, finally going off to sea on a merchant ship. At Jamaica he ran away, and, associating himself with some other reckless characters, they stole a canoe, and went to Grand Cayman, hoping there to meet with others of their ilk, who were reputed to use that island as a base when they were looking for opportunities to join a pirate crew.

Finding some likely comrades, they made up a company of 20 men, captured a turtling sloop, and set out in search of booty. After taking a prize, Howard made for Madagascar, living at St. Augustine for a time. He was reputed to have eventually settled on the coast of India, where he married a local girl and became a wealthy man. Howard is perhaps, therefore, that rare example of a man who started out on the wrong foot, but did not live to bitterly regret his days of youthful pirating, unless, in his eastern outpost, he suffered the nostalgia of an exile from home. [33]

PIRACY IN CAYMAN:
THE EXPLOITS OF NEAL WALKER

Cayman's treacherous reefs have caused innumerable wrecks. The opportunities afforded for salvage were not lost upon inhabitants, who, as the islands came to be permanently settled, increasingly made a livelihood from the hulks and cargoes of those vessels unfortunate enough to run aground off Cayman. Wrecks could also tempt individuals into acts of piracy, as Neal Walker's story demonstrates.

When the Genoesa was wrecked on Pedro's Point shoals in 1731, Walker, an inhabitant of Jamaica, and master of a sloop, was employed by the ship's agent to go in search of the President of Panama and other dignitaries reported to have been travelling on her and who had escaped on a raft. However, contrary to his instructions, he "*stopt at the wrack, fish'd up as considerable quantity of Treasure which he carry'd with him and has not been heard of since*".

When another vessel, the 'St Michael', was also wrecked in Cayman, Neal Walker was again involved in her plunder. Edward Pratter and James Rigby, agents of the Assiento Company, complained to the Council of Jamaica that Walker had,"*in the months of November and December last made two several voyages to the Little Camanas and plundered from the Brigne St Michael lately stranded on the said Camanas and belonging to the subjects of His Catholick Majesty, great quantitys of wine brandy etc*".

All enquiries with British colonies which the agents had made, having proved fruitless, they noted:

> we apprehend he conceals himself in some place near this island and probably if His Majesty's most gracious pardon could be obtain'd for the said Neal Walker and his crew, upon their coming into port and delivering to your Petitioners for the Benefit of His Catholick Majesty all the gold and silver plundered from the said wreck St Michael, the said Neal Walker would readily embrace the said most gracious pardon, and thereby His Catholick Majesty might recover a considerable sum and this Island be free from the danger of the said Neal Walker if he should be driven to pursue his evil courses.

A few weeks later, a letter was received, which informed the Jamaican authorities that Walker had admitted plundering the Genovesa, together with another vessel, stealing from it more than 60,000 pieces of eight which the two crews had divided equally between them. Walker and his men now "pray'd a pardon at Jamaica for their lives and would return to the King of Spain his Master everything that they had carry'd from the wreck of the said ship".

Whilst the Spanish were simply anxious to recover their property, the local authorities, were concerned with the effect a pardon would have, and declared themselves unanimously of opinion that *"he ought not to be pardon'd because, if his offence be piracy it must be of very ill consequence to pardon him, and not sufficiently deter others from committing the like crimes, and tend only to encourage pirates and should not his offence be piracy, a pardon from the King can be of no effect to him so as to barr the subject or sufferers from the civil remedy given them by law"*. [34]

Attitudes to piracy had undergone a sea-change from the heady days of privateering under Morgan and his ilk when the embryonic, ill-defended settlements of the British in the Caribbean preferred to treat with renegades rather than face attack from their enemies. Jamaica, Barbados, Bermuda, the Bahamas and the American colonies, were by the 1720s and 1730s, determined to stamp out the scourge of piracy which threatened their trade, terrorised their most respectable citizens, and was a source of temptation to their most youthful, underpaid and underemployed populations of mariners, and servants and even to their slaves. They met their tormentors with the ferocity of their naval fire power and the unwelcome sight of the gallows. Scores of executions, and the exhibition of mutilated bodies and severed heads, made these colonies awash with the blood of pirates, before their last stand was finally over.

REFERENCES

1. C. Johnson, *A General History of the Pirates*, p. 21; M. Rediker, *Between the Devil and the Deep Blue Sea*, p 267-8. The other group was centred on Lowther and Low whose crews met in Cayman.
2. PRO CO 152/12/2 no 67 (iii) deposition of Henry Bostock ; and see CSP Aug 1717-Dec 1718 no. 298 Governor Hamilton to Council of Trade and Plantations 6 Jan 1718.
3. CSP Aug 1717-Dec 1718 no 551 Lt Governor Bennett, Bermuda to Council of Trade and Plantations, 31 May 1718: Governor Johnson, Charles Town, South Carolina to Council of Trade and Plantations; see also PRO CO 5/1265 no 106 and CO 5/1293 pp 154-7; CSP 1717-18 no 556 Governor Johnson, Charles Town, South Carolina to Council of Trade and Plantations, 18 June 1718; No 800 Governor Spotswood, Virginia, 22 Dec 1718 to Council of Trade and Plantations.
4. CSP 1717-18 no 730 Governor and Council of South Carolina to the Council of Trade and Plantations, 21 Oct 1718.
5. ibid., no 787 Governor and Council of South Carolina to the Council of Trade and Plantations, 12 December 1718; No 800 Governor Spotswood, Virginia, 22 Dec 1718 to Council of Trade and Plantations.
6. PRO ADM 1/1472 Captains' Letters 1717-1723; Lyme, Virginia, 6 Feb 1718/19; ADM 41/4250 Captain's Log HMS Lyme.
7. Jameson, J.F. *Privateering and Piracy in the Colonial Period: Illustrative Documents*, p. 323-355.
8. Chapin, H.M. *Privateer Ships and Sailors, the first century of American colonial privateering, 1625-1725*, p. 236-7; Oliver, op. cit., p. 28.
9. C. Johnson, op.cit.,p. 72-79; D. Cordingley, *Life among the pirates*, p. 189; see also PRO CO 137/14, depositions at the trial of Vane and his crew.
10. CSP Aug 1717-Dec 1718 no 551 (p 260-264) Lt Governor Bennett, Bermuda to Council of Trade and Plantations, 31 May 1718; CO 37/10 Enclosure i Deposition of Samuel Cooper, 24 May 1718.
11. CSP 1717-18 no 737 Governor Woodes Rogers to the Council of Trade and Plantations, Nassau on Providence, 31 Oct 1718.
12. PRO CO 137/14 Deposition of Hosea Tisdall.
13. Cordingley, p. 101, p. 172.
14. C. Johnson, op. cit., p. 80-85; see also CO 137/14 for depositions made at the trials of Vane and Rackam.
15. PRO CO 137/14 Deposition of Thomas Spenlow.
16. CSP 1720-21 no 340 Governor Lawes to the Council of Trade and Plantations, 28 December 1720.

17. C. Johnson, op. cit., p. 94-96.
18. Such was the interest in the trials of these pirates, that the transcripts were printed. Copies were sent to London with the Governor's despatch of 12 June 1721: CSP 1720-21, no 523 Lawes to the Council of Trade and Plantations. See PRO CO 137/14 for the original trial transcripts of Anne Bonny and Mary Read
19. C. Johnson, op. cit., p. 86-93.
20. PRO CO 137/14 see the depositions of Thomas Dillon and Dorothy Thomas.
21. C. Johnson, op. cit., p. 271-285.
22. G. Dow and J. Edmonds, *The Pirates of the New England Coast*, p 231.
23. CSP 1724-5 no 102 Governor Hart to the Council of Trade and Plantations, 25 March 1724.
24. CSP 1722-3 No 606 Governor Burnet (New York) to Lord Carteret, 25 June 1723.
25 PRO CO 28/18 Depositions of John Wickstead, Goldsmith Blowers, John Crawford and Benjamin Flint; see also CSP 1722-3 no 754 Governor Worsley to Council of Trade and Plantations, 24 Nov 1723.
26. PRO CO 152-14 The Tryal of Robert Corp and Henry Wynn for Piracy 11th March 1724; and see Walter Moore's Deposition.
27. CSP 17244-5 no 8 Worsley to Carteret, 11 Jan 1724 and PRO CO 28/44 Depositions of Hunt and Rosario, nos 65 (i) and 65 (vi).
28. CSP 1720-1 no 758 Governor Phenney to Council of Trade and Plantations, 26 Dec 1721.
29. CSP 1722-3 no 333 Order of Committee of Council 13 Nov 1722. 30. C. Johnson, op. cit., p. 255-262.
31. CSP 1722-3 no 444 Hope to the Council of Trade and Plantations, 21 Feb 1723.
32. C. Johnson, op. cit., p. 303-304.
33. B. Ebanks, *Cayman Emerges* p. 22; see also R.S. Smith, op. cit., p. 110.
34. PRO CO 137/54 Governor Hunter to the Duke of Newcastle, 18 Jan 1732, enclosing Minutes of Council, 6 April 1731 and 11 May 1731; and see CSP 1733 no 22.

Edward Low as depicted in *The Pirates' Own Book*, 1842

**Blackbeard's fight with Lieutenant Maynard,
as visualised in *The Pirates' Own Book*, 1842**

CHAPTER FIVE

THE PIRATE LEGACY IN CAYMAN

Like many of the American seaboard towns and Caribbean islands which depended on their ocean-going trade and skills, Caymanians remain very aware and proud of their maritime heritage. Privateers and corsairs were the celebrities of their day – their courage and daring the toast of seaside taverns. The depredations caused by corsairs and pirates long forgotten, their exploits are today remembered only in annual festivities such as Pirates Week, which plunges Cayman into several days of colourful pageantry each October. The pirate theme can also be enjoyed by visitors all year round in the several pubs and restaurants which recall the swashbuckling age of the buccaneer. For the souvenir hunter, or the lover of ancient artefacts, a real piece of pirate history can even be purchased in Cayman, from one of the treasure shops which sell doubloons and other coins salvaged from wrecked ships around the islands. And the serious searcher of the pirate legacy can even explore the underwater and underground sites where pirate battles were once fought, and where pirates, or terrified inhabitants, may have hidden.

PIRATE SITES

Localities on Grand Cayman which have a link with the pirate heritage include **Bodden Town**, where natural limestone caves are said to have been used by villagers to conceal themselves from attack, **West Bay** and **Seven Mile Beach** where buccaneers like Dampier anchored to look for fresh water, and to collect turtles, and **North Sound**, which was used as a careening place for visiting ships.

THE PIRATE CAVES

The pirate caves in Bodden Town are a lively tourist attraction. The venue comprises an attractive and educational garden which displays some of the interesting flora and fauna of the Cayman Islands, as well as the caves themselves which are surprisingly extensive and spooky. The owners have placed a number of artefacts in the caves designed to recreate the pirate ambiance. Some are amusing, others are gruesome, and no doubt a pretty accurate portrayal of the violent and sometimes squalid life of the 17th century pirates who are believed to have come here.

There is also an old style Cayman house to visit, a tree house, a convenient hammock to rest in, a souvenir shop, and often traditional Caymanian cuisine on offer.

PIRATE GRAVES

Across the road from the caves in Bodden Town, a small graveyard on the sea-side is said to include some of the last resting places of the pirates who reputedly frequented this part of the island. The names are no longer legible, but given the origins of early settlers, it is not implausible that pirates, or their descendants, are buried here.

PIRATE SOUVENIRS

PIECES OF EIGHT
AND OTHER TREASURE SOUVENIRS

One of the more unique souvenirs which can be purchased in the Cayman Islands is a historic coin, such as a Spanish doubloon. In recent years, there have been numerous attempts to salvage treasure from the many wrecked ships around the Cayman Islands. Local Caymanians who assisted in such treasure hunts were often paid in found coins. Sometimes, islanders would wear their pieces of eight around their necks on a leather strap, and with a bezel fashioned around the coin. Visitors naturally wanted to obtain such a valuable curio for themselves, and today there are a number of venues on the islands where tourists can learn about these historic coins, purchase one of these valuable souvenirs, and even create their own item of coin jewellery.

DUTY FREE LTD.

At **Duty Free**, on the George Town waterfront (next to the Hard Rock Café) Michel Lemay is usually on hand to explain aspects of the fascinating coin history of the region, and to show visitors Spanish gold doubloons, Pieces of Eight (Spanish silver coins) and even Greek and Roman coins. With over 15years experience in the field, and a member of the American Numismatic Association, Michael Lemay is highly regarded for his knowledge and integrity. The coins at Duty Free are all purchased directly from treasure hunters, or acquired from coin brokers and auction houses such as Christie's, Sotheby's, Ponterio and U.B.S. to name a few. All coins are supplied with a certificate of authenticity.

Duty Free has an extensive collection of historic coins which have been recovered from shipwrecks, buried treasure and obtained from private collections. In addition, a superb selection of set coins in 14 and 18 carat gold, with or without gemstones, are also available. Most settings for the coins are carefully designed by Michel himself and manufactured in the Cayman Islands by Island Companies Ltd.

Michel Lemay of Duty Free, displays a treasure coin.

A visit to Duty Free on the Waterfront is both an educational and an enjoyable experience. Visitors can profit from Michel Lemay's evident expertise in this fascinating area, whilst viewing doubloons, pieces of eight, and other delightful coins which most of us have only heard about from books and films, but never seen. Choosing a unique piece of coin jewellery or an original treasure coin while learning about their memorable past will be an experience that most visitors will cherish for years to come.

CHAPTER FIVE

THE PIRATE LEGACY IN CAYMAN

PIRATE CRUISES

Visitors to the island during the October Pirates' Week festivities can effect a pirate landing and carouse with appropriately dressed revellers. But for an all-year round pirate experience, a cruise on the Jolly Roger is unbeatable. As soon as you step on board, the crew, brandishing their cutlasses, and cussing loudly ply you with alcoholic drinks in true pirate fashion. The cruise around Cayman in the fascinating replica pirate ship with its olde style cables and rigging, is an unmissable step into the island's maritime past.

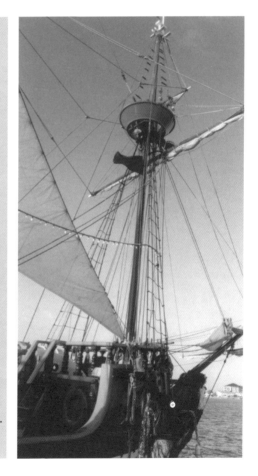

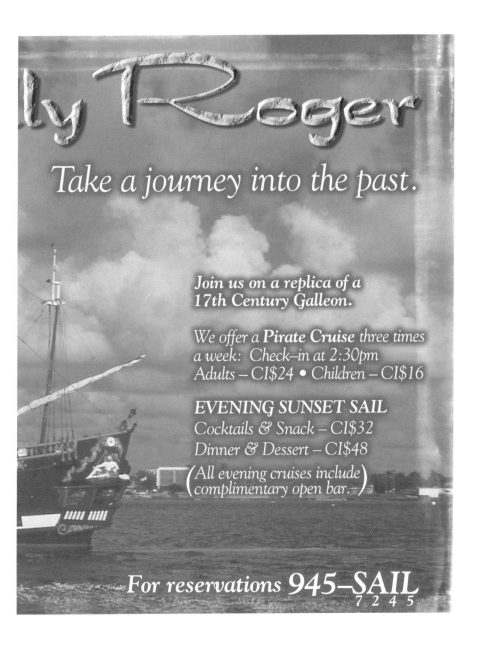

LITTLE CAYMAN'S PIRATE HERITAGE

While cutlasses have been recovered from the mangroves of North Sound on Grand Cayman, and coins have at times been unearthed on the shore and in caves, the greatest archaeological finds have been discovered around Little Cayman.

A survey in the waters off **South Hole Sound**, Little Cayman have recently uncovered a wrecksite believed to be the remains of one of the armed sloops attacked by the corsair Rivero Pardal in 1669. Tobacco pipes, a lead musket ball, a Spanish olive jar and other 17th century artefacts have also been found there.

A well near **Jackson's Point**, on Little Cayman is known to locals as the 'pirates well', and seems to have been in use for more than two centuries. It was searched by archaelogists who found "cultural debris such as ceramic fragments, tobacco pipes and bottles as well as buttons. Analysis of these materials suggests that the water source was used for at least two hundred years.

CAYMAN BRAC'S PIRATE ARTEFACTS

Spanish silver coins and a clock manufactured in Barcelona in 1729 are among the artefacts which have been found on the Brac. Visitors to any of the islands' coves and caves, and particularly on less well developed Brac and Little Cayman may have the good fortune to unearth yet more of the pirate booty which is surely still waiting somewhere on these shores to be discovered ....

CONCLUSION

The Cayman Islands were, until recently, sparsely settled and isolated outposts in the Caribbean sea. Early visitors to the islands, however, noted the abundance of marine life and soon the facility of obtaining provisions at Cayman led to their increasing use by passing ships. But it was not only ordinary seamen who came to avail of the natural resources of the Cayman Islands. Pirates were always on the look-out for a quiet retreat where they could stock up on supplies, repair their vessels and keep watch for likely booty in the form of richly laden passing merchant ships. The quiet coves of Cayman seemed ideal.

By the early 1700s when the most notorious of the pirates called in at Cayman, the islands had already attracted sporadic settlements. The numbers of inhabitants fluctuated as shipwrecks and other adventures deposited human flotsam on its beaches, to be picked up again by visiting turtlers and provisioning ships. The few settlers in their simple lodgings were constantly engaged in a struggle for survival, and were no match for the marauders who habitually invaded their shores. On the contrary, seeing the approach of pirate ships, the settlers were more likely to flee into makeshift huts established for the purpose in the wooded interior of Grand Cayman. The pirates had a free hand to careen their sloops and deplete the stores looted from their victims.

After 1661 Cayman was considered to be part of English-run Jamaica and the settlers were fair game for their rivals – the Spanish and the Portuguese. Raids were common. An attack by the corsair Rivero on 1669 was answered by Morgan's attack on the city of Panama, but Cayman had been shown to be vulnerable, its settlers were recalled to Jamaica, and the islands were to remain at the mercy of passing pirates for many years to come. Thus it was that the heterogeneous pirate crews who cruised the Caribbean in the 17th century and the early years of the 18th century, who interspersed voyages of plunder with binges of hard drinking and brawling, came to see Cayman as their own domain.

Piracy and privateering have played a significant role in the history of the Cayman Islands and cannot be lightly forgotten. There is little doubt that they were among the early settlers of these isles and that more than a little buccaneers' blood courses through the veins of modern Caymanians. Yet piracy was a scourge, feared by all who depended on the ocean for transport and trade. From humble fisher folk to fabulously wealthy merchants, all lived in fear of the raising of the trademark black and red flags which forewarned of a pirate attack. It is a mistake to glamourize the figure of the pirate, and this volume has attempted instead faithfully to portray the violence, squalor and brutishly short lives of the more notorious of the pirates who haunted Cayman shores in days gone by.

While some pirates were guilty of appalling torture, and even celebrated privateers like Henry Morgan were criticised for their brutality in the sacking of enemy cities, the actions of the brigands must be seen in the context of the times. State sponsored torture was very widespread in the 17th century. Governments in Europe routinely used the rack and other devices similar to those used by pirates to extract confessions from prisoners. Burnings – of suspected witches, for example – and hanging of petty criminals was common. The violence to which the pirates' bodies were themselves exposed is evidence of the methods used to deal with transgressors. In an era when men could be press ganged into joining the navy, and subjected to horrific punishments for minor misdemeanours on board HM ships, prey to the sadism of superior officers, and their fellow mariners, it cannot be wondered at that some of these brutalised sailors should have deserted to form pirate crews where a greater spirit of egalitarianism prevailed, or that they sometimes sought revenge against their tormentors should they chance upon them. Indeed, the mock trials which pirates such as Captain Anstis reportedly held, indicates that these men were consciously rejecting the values of their age, and mocking the very loyalties which men held dear.

It should also be remembered that in the frontier societies of the Caribbean, the rule of law was far from entrenched. The musket and the sword took the place of policeman and judge, and in the struggle for survival, as Scott famously commented, the life of a man in Cayman might be worth no more than a brace of wood-pigeon.

While reliving the past in the swashbuckling celebrations of the present, we should spare a thought for the men whose job it was to hunt down and capture notorious villains like Blackbeard, it is perhaps they who should be glorified, rather than the pirates themselves. Finally, we should remember the victims of piracy, many of them Caymanians, who suffered the scourge of raids, arson attacks, looting and pillage for more than two centuries.

THE FATEFUL MOMENT: MUTINY ABOARD SHIP
(Hazel, The Flying Yankee, 1928)

GLOSSARY

Boatswain Officer of a ship in charge of sails, rigging, anchors etc.

Bowsprit A heavy spar pointing forward from the front of a ship.

Brigantine A two-masted vessel with fully square-rigged foremast, fore-and-aft rigged main mast and square sails on main topmast.

Buccaneer A term for hunters on Hispaniola, also used for privateers and pirates of the West Indies and American coasts from 1650.

Caravel Small and light sailing ship, popular in Spain and Portugal from the 15th-17th centuries.

Careen Cleaning a heeled-over ship.

Fore-and-aft At bow and stern.

Man of War A 3 square rigged vessel usually over 300 tons employed as a naval vessel.

Mizzenmast Mast at the back of a vessel.

Pinnace Small two masted ship.

Privateer Armed vessel authorised by commission or 'letters of marque' to attack enemy ships.

Roads area of water just outside a main harbour where ships can anchor.

Schooner shallow draught sailing vessel, usually with two masts.

Ship Usually designating a vessel with three or more masts and fully square-rigged

Sloop small single masted and easily manoeuvrable sailing boat.

Spanish Main name for the Spanish Empire in the New World. First applied to the mainland, the term came to include the West Indian islands and Caribbean waters traversed by Spanish treasure fleets.

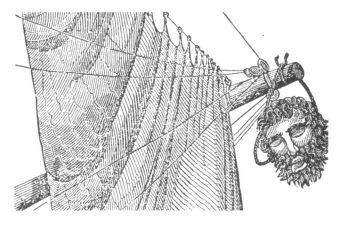

Blackbeard's severed head dangles from the **bowsprit**

FURTHER READING

MANUSCRIPT SOURCES

Manuscript documents, including pirates' trials, petitions, and the reports and statements of naval officers and seamen who were witness to acts of piracy, can be read at the Public Records Office (PRO), Kew, London, chiefly in the Colonial Office (CO) and Admiralty (ADM) series. A useful printed summary of many manuscript sources can be found in the Calendar of State Papers, (CSP) available in archives and good libraries. Contemporary gazettes and newsletters, such as the *Boston News,* also contain detailed references to pirate captures and trials. The Cayman Islands National Archive (CINA) has a useful collection of archival holdings from around the world, including translations of Spanish (AGI) documents.

CONTEMPORARY PRINTED SOURCES

Piracy was a subject which captured the attention of 17th century readers, as much as it does today. People were anxious to read of the exploits of their privateer heroes, and the roguish pirates alike. There are accordingly a number of delightful sources dating from the 17th and 18th centuries, which must however be read with caution, as what purport to be true narratives of eye witnesses, or credible histories, may in parts be plagiarised or sheer fabrication.

A selection of the best accounts include:

Bigges, W. *Sir Francis Drake's West Indian Voyage*, London, 1589 (1969 edn).

Du Tertre J.B., *Histoire generale des Antilles Habitee par les Francais*, 4 vols, Paris 1667-71.

Johnson, C. *A General History of the Pirates*, (first edition 1724) 1926 edition George Routledge & Sons, (ed A.L. Hayward).

Laet, Johannes de *History of the West India Company*, 1931-7 edition. (translation of the Latin original of 1633).

Masefield, J. (ed.) *Dampier's Voyages*, London, 1906.

Oexmelin, A.O. *Buccaniers of America*, 1684.

Sloane, Hans *A Voyage to the Island Madera, Barbados, Nieves, S. Christophers and Jamaica*, 2 vols, London, 1707.

Thomson, G.A. *Alcedo's Geographical Dictionary*, London, 1812.

SECONDARY SOURCES

A list of the 19th and 20th century works by historians on pirates and privateers which have been used in the compilation of this book is given below:

Andrews, K.R. (ed) *English Privateering Voyages to the West Indies, 1588-95*, CUP, 1959.

Blond, G. *Histoire de la Flibuste*, 2nd edn Stock, 1990.

Bromley, J.S. *Corsairs and Navies, 1660-1760*, London, 1987.

Chapin, H.M. *Privateer Ships and Sailors, the first century of American colonial privateering, 1625-1725*, 1926, France.

Dow, G.F. & Edmonds, J.H. *The Pirates of the New England Coast, 1630-1730*, Salem, 1923.

Earle, P. *The Sack of Panama*, 1981.

Haring, C.H. *The Buccaneers in the West Indies in the XVII Century*, 1910.

Hirst, G.S.S. *Notes on the History of the Cayman Islands*, Kingston, Jamaica, 1910.

Jameson, J.F. *Privateering and Piracy in the Colonial Period: Illustrative Documents,* New York, 1923.

Johnson, S. *Sunken Ships and Treasures*, Macmillan USA, 2000.

Keeler, M. Frear, *Sir Francis Drake's West Indian Voyage 1585-86*, Hakluyt Society, 1981.

Kemp, P.K. & Lloyd, C. *The Brethren of the Coast*, 1960, London.

Lane, K.E. *Blood and Silver A History of Piracy in the Caribbean and Central America*, Signal Books, UK, 1999.

Morison, S.E. *Journals and Other Documents on the Life and Voyages of Christopher Columbus*, 1963

Oliver, M. *Blackbeard and his murderous mateys*, Miles Kelly Publishing, 2000.

Pascall, J. *Pirates and Privateers*, Samson Low, 1978.

Pawson, M. & Buisseret, D. *Port Royal, Jamaica*, Oxford, 1975.

Pickford, N. *The Atlas of Ship Wreck & Treasure*, 1994, London.

Rediker, M *Between the Devil and the Deep Blue Sea*, Cambridge, 1987.

Shuter, J. *Exquemelin and the Pirates of the Caribbean*, Heinemann, Oxford, 1993.

Ure, J. *The Quest for Captain Morgan*, London 1983.